Interpreting Drama

Interpreting Drama

PRABHANJAN MANE

ATLANTIC

PUBLISHERS & DISTRIBUTORS (P) LTD

Published by
ATLANTIC
PUBLISHERS & DISTRIBUTORS (P) LTD
7/22, Ansari Road, Darya Ganj,
New Delhi-110002
Phones : +91-11-40775252, 23273880, 23275880, 23280451
Fax : +91-11-23285873
Web : www.atlanticbooks.com
E-mail : orders@atlanticbooks.com

Branch Office
5, Nallathambi Street, Wallajah Road,
Chennai-600002
Phones : +91-44-64611085, 32413319
E-mail : chennai@atlanticbooks.com

ISBN 978-81-269-1348-0

Printed in India at Nice Printing Press, A-33/3A, Site-IV, Industrial Area, Sahibabad, Ghaziabad, U.P.

Acknowledgements

For the completion of this book, I would like to express my deep and sincere gratitude, first of all, to my supervisor, Dr. Prashant K. Sinha, for his help, support, and most of all, infinite patience. His pursuit of excellence spurred me on to put in my best always. Working with him was a pleasure. He was a constant source of gentle encouragement. I specially thank him for his encouragement in carrying out this study, by providing in himself a living example of dedicated scholarship for me to emulate.

My sincere and heartfelt thanks are due to Dr. K.S. Iyer, my teacher, who helped me whenever I approached him. I am deeply obliged to him for his valuable advice and suggestions.

Finally, I would like to thank my father for his tremendous moral support and constant encouragement in my research. I am indebted to my mother for her continued support, care and affection. She created for me a peaceful atmosphere in which I could work without tension. I am also grateful to my wife and brother without whose love, support and much-needed encouragement I would not have been able to complete this work.

Prabhanjan Mane

Foreword

Prabhanjan Mane, in his book on drama—meant primarily for students of English Literature at the university level—has addressed issues of cardinal significance to the Indian academia. In our ardour to teach drama as "literature", we approach it, as we would a novel and lose sight of the fact that a play is meant to be staged. Certain issues, distinctly unrelated to the study and teaching of fiction are central to the discipline of drama. Thus, one aspect of any analysis of drama is the relationship between the stage and the audience and the related feature of what Aristotle in his *Poetics* described as "spectacle." The Attic theatre, therefore, did not have a proscenium stage. The performers were separated from the audience by masks which also incidentally served as megaphones. The properties were simple, minimal and unsophisticated. In late Elizabethan and Jacobean theatres, curtains had been introduced, and the stage was more elaborate with its three floors, the projecting part in front of the apron, the study, the chamber, the balcony, the cellar and the "heavens". Moreover, there was now a varied equation between the actors and the audiences as the soliloquies and the direct addresses by the former to the latter introduced greater intimacy and interaction between them.

With the reopening of the theatres in 1660, the boundaries between the stage and the auditorium were more sharply drawn. Nevertheless, features like the Prologue and the Epilogue did involve another level of interaction across the curtain. However, the rise of realism or naturalism in the late 19th century 'with its concept of the transparent fourth wall in its desire for verisimilitude' divided the stage and the auditorium into two watertight compartments. In fact, theatrically, the actors in a middle or late Ibsen or in a Chekhov play are oblivious of the presence of the people in the hall. However, a breach was made in the wall by Pirandello and those who followed him, like Genet. When in Pirandello, the six characters enter the hall and walk through the audience to the stage or when in the same play, the producer goes down into the hall to view the "rehearsal" on the stage, they obliterate the distinction between the two worlds. Similarly, in Genet's *Balcony*, when Madame Irma announces that she is turning off the lights and invites the audience to come back again or in Peter Weiss's *Marat/Sade*, when the male nurses of the lunatic asylum chase the patients running away into the midst of the audience, there is a strange interaction between the two worlds. Thus, the emotional involvement of the audience watching *Hedda Gabler* or *The Master Builder* or *The Seagull* benefits from the total refusal of the actors to acknowledge them, whereas the changing relationship between the stage and the auditorium in a Pirandello or a Molnar or a Genet play simply punctures the illusion and puts the audience in a detached frame of mind. Now this is an aspect of drama that is non-existent in fiction, and the teacher teaching drama as if it were a novel, would completely miss this point. It is to the credit of Prabhanjan Mane that he has tried to highlight the fact that drama is meant for performance.

Mane's rather multifaceted study of drama as a form furnishes us with elaborate analyses of various concepts of character and techniques of characterization. Although several schools of recent critical theory have launched a frontal assault on the tradition of character study, there can be no denying the fact that in theatre with a human actor embodying a character—an iconic mode—it is preposterous to think of characters as merely "words on a page". A.C. Bradley may have gone too far in examining figures in Shakespearean tragedy as full-fledged human beings, and L.C. Knights was not entirely mistaken in denouncing this trend in his ridicule of those who wondered how many children Lady Macbeth had. Nevertheless, in drama, characters are vibrant "personalities", and it is worthwhile on the part of Mane to explore the topic in depth. He has competently illustrated his approach with a thorough analysis of characters, among other plays, in *Othello*, which by introducing the issue of race, goes beyond *Hamlet*, *Lear* and *Macbeth*.

The concept of "structure" has hardly been understood by Indian students, who in their answers on plot tend to summarise the story of the play. Mane's book is a right step in the direction of inviting them to attend to the shape of a play as distinct from its contents. Examining plays which are as differently constructed as *Dr. Faustus*, *Death of a Salesman*, and *Antigone*, he dwells upon a spectrum of structures from the interior journey in *Death of a Salesman* to the linear movement in *Dr. Faustus*. One issue that needs some more elaboration is that of the subplot, often viewed as a cardinal strength of plays variously spread across centuries like *Hamlet*, *King Lear*, *The Misanthrope*, *She Stoops to Conquer*, *Man and Superman* and *The Cherry Orchard*. As it were, it is here that plays and novels evince such marked resemblances. Just as the story of Gloucester and his two sons illuminates the events in the family of King Lear, Tolstoy's Kitty and Levin highlight the situation of Anna, Vronsky and Karenin. If the predicaments of Fortinbras and Laertes suggest striking parallels to that of Hamlet, so do the twists and turns in the affair of Jane and Bingley reflecting on the relationship of Darcy and Elizabeth.

Our students also tend to ignore the significance of imagery in prose drama. Thanks to studies like G. Wilson Knight's, we do attend to imagery in verse drama, especially of Elizabethan and Jacobean periods. However, many prose works also contain elaborate imagistic structures. Can we ignore land and water imagery in *A Man for All Seasons* or all the references to buildings in *The Master Builder*? The students and enthusiasts of drama have to pay attention to factors like the repetition as well as the development of images. Moreover, different characters may use the same image with different meanings in mind. In fact, some of the central images are multivalent. Thus, in *The Seagull* Nina and Trogorin see "he" as the seagull, whereas for Trepliov, it is not "her" but "he himself" who is the seagull. This leads us to a seminal feature of dramatic imagery: the fact that so many of the dominant images in drama are visual symbols and the dialogue only reinforces the object on the stage. Thus, *The Wild Duck* (never directly seen by the audience) and *The Cherry Orchard* (again in the eponymous play), the house(s) in *The Three Sisters* and *The Ghost Sonata* and the wagon in Brecht's *Mother Courage and Her Children* are wonderful illustrations of dominant stage symbols with varying degrees of reinforcement from dialogues.

In a play, the atmosphere or the mood is evoked in ways that differ from those in fiction. Music, sound effects, the scene, the seasons, the time of day—all contribute to the atmosphere in *The Three Sisters*. So do the shadows cast on the floor by the stained glass windows, the sounds in the garden, the play of light and shade, and the isolated locale of the chateau in Maeterlinck's *The Intruder*. Thus, the non-verbal means, which are effectively translated on the stage in terms of powerful visual and auditory appeals, enhance the mood of the play. This is certainly not how Katherine Mansfield creates the atmosphere in her stories or D.H. Lawrence evokes it in *The Fox*. The extraordinary description of the night outside when Mrs. Morel is turned out of the house by her husband Walter is entirely, as is logical in a novel, through verbal description. In contrast, Maeterlinck in *Pelleas and Melisanda* evokes nature in the night through visual means and direct appeal to the senses.

Prabhanjan Mane, by highlighting the salient features of drama as a genre, has tried to fulfil a deeply felt need of students of drama. He has also confined his illustrations, on the whole, to plays normally taught in the institutions in his region. In some ways, this limits the range of his intended readership but on the other hand, it caters, in a more concrete manner, to a specific audience with a local habitation and a name.

I hope students find reading this book an enjoyable, stimulating and enriching experience, and are inspired to pursue "gems of purest ray serene" in the inexhaustible treasure house of drama.

Prashant K. Sinha

Contents

1

Introduction

Drama Defined. A play is a literary work or a composition which delineates life and human activity by means of presenting various actions of—and dialogues among—a group of characters. Drama is furthermore designed for theatrical presentation, i.e. although we speak of a play as a literary work or a composition, we must never forget that drama is designed to be acted on the stage. When we read a play, we have no real grasp of what that play is like unless we at least attempt to imagine how actors on a stage would present the material. There are a few plays which are basically meant for reading rather than for theatrical performance and these are referred to as "closet dramas". For the most part, then, we are talking about drama as a vehicle for "live" presentation on the stage and although we may find ourselves wandering discursively into abstract considerations of imagery and irony, we should keep before us at all times the principle that the success of a drama must be somewhat based on the way it "works" in the theatre. Finally, drama is more than the representation of life and character through action and dialogue, for drama is also entertainment. While this term is subject—and has been subjected—to various definitions, everyone agrees that entertainment is nevertheless one of the ostensible objectives of drama.

HISTORY OF DRAMA IN THE WEST

Before turning our attention to particular aspects of drama, as well as to particular plays, it seems worthwhile to survey briefly the development of drama as a generic form, i.e. when we speak of drama as a *genre*, we must be aware of the different forms of the *genre* that has evolved over several thousand years. A Roman play is a long way from a Restoration Comedy in both temperament and form. And just as all plays are different, so they are all the same—for they all try to capture moments of life. This is why William Butler Yeats felt that drama is the epitome of all the arts; as he explained, "What attracts me to drama is that it is, in the most obvious way what all the arts are upon a last analysis. A farce and a tragedy are alike in this, that they are a moment of intense life." Let us explore briefly some of the ways in which dramatists have used the form for capturing moments of life.

The Beginnings. First and foremost it should be noted that Western drama commenced with religious celebrations: out of the various pagan rites and festivals arose the earliest dramas of an entertaining kind, specifically, Greek Tragedy and Greek Comedy.

Greek Theatre. The first evidence of dramatic literature dates from Greece in the 6th century BC, and the first extant piece of critical writing on the origin of theatre is Aristotle's *Poetics* (c. 330 BC). Aristotle claimed that Greek tragedy developed from dithyrambs—choral hymns in honour of the God Dionysus—which not only praised the god but often told a story. According to legend, Thespis, a choral leader of the 6th century BC, created drama when he assumed the part of the leading character in a dithyrambic story: he spoke and the chorus responded. From this it was but a small step to the addition of other actors and characters and the evolution of drama as an independent form, according to Aristotle. But the seemingly spontaneous development of highly sophisticated tragic drama with virtually no precedents is difficult to explain.

Greek tragedy flourished in the 5th century BC. Of more than 1,000 tragedies written during that century, only 31 remain, all by Aeschylus, Sophocles, and Euripides—the best known being the Orestian trilogy by Aeschylus, *Oedipus Rex* and *Antigone* by Sophocles and *Hippolytus* by Euripides. The plays are highly formal, they are written in verse and consist of scenes (episodes) among characters (never more than three speaking characters in a scene) alternating with choral songs (odes). The stories are mostly drawn from myth or ancient history, although the focus is not on a simple retelling of a story (with which the poets often took liberties), yet on a consideration of humanity's place in the world and the consequences of individual actions. Generally, little action occurred onstage and most events and information were related through dialogue and choral songs.

The plays were presented at festivals in honour of Dionysus, including the Great Dionysia at Athens, held in spring; the Rural Dionysia, held in winter; and the Lenaea, also held in the winter following the Rural Dionysia. The works of only three poets, selected in competition, were performed. In addition to three tragic plays (a trilogy) each poet had to present a satyr play—a farcical, often bawdy parody of the gods and their myths. Later, comedy, which developed in the mid-5th century BC, was also presented. The oldest extant comedies are by Aristophanes. They have a highly formal structure thought to be derived from ancient fertility rites. The humour consists of a mixture of satirical attacks on contemporary public figures, bawdy, scatological jokes, and seemingly sacrilegious parodies of the gods. By the 4th century BC comedy had supplanted tragedy as the dominant form.

As Greek culture spread in the wake of the conquests of Alexander the Great, the topical, literary comedies and philosophical tragedies became inappropriate, and domestic comedy—called Middle and New Comedy—proliferated. Only one complete New Comedy survives—the *Dyskolos* (317 BC; The Curmudgeon or The Misanthrope) by Menander. These plays are similar in plot and style to the situation comedies on television today. The plot hinges on a complication or situation revolving around love, family problems, money, or the like.

The characters are stock—identifiable, simplified social types, such as a miserly father or a nagging mother-in-law.

The form of the Greek physical theatre evolved over two centuries; interestingly, the permanent stone theatres that survive today as ruins were not built until the 4th century BC, i.e. after the classical period of playwriting. The open-air theatres may have consisted of an orchestra—a flat circular area used for choral dances—a raised stage behind it for actors, and a roughly semi-circular seating area built into a hillside around the orchestra, although modern scholars debate the layout of particular theatres. These theatres held 15,000 to 20,000 spectators. As the importance of actors grew and that of the chorus diminished, the stage became higher and encroached on the orchestra space.

The actors—all men—wore theatricalized versions of everyday dress, but, most importantly, they wore larger-than-life masks, which aided visibility and indicated the nature of the character to the audience. In the vast theatres, subtle gestures and facial expressions, upon which modern actors depend, would have been lost. Movement was apparently stately and formal, and the greatest emphasis was on the voice. Music accompanied the dances. An ancient Greek production was probably more akin to opera than to modern drama.

In keeping with its religious function, the theatre was state supported, admission was free or nominal to everyone, and actors were highly regarded. Working at the same time were the mimes—male and female popular entertainers who plied their trade wherever an audience would toss a few coins.

Tragedy and Comedy Contrasted. Because the beginnings of all dramatic history are grounded in the fundamental categories of comedy and tragedy, it is worthwhile to establish the essential differences and similarities existing between them. Tragedy involves events which climax in unhappy disaster, while comedy deals with events which inevitably find some sort of pleasing or happy resolution; tragedy then, as explained by the subject matter itself, is necessarily dark while comedy, also in subject matter, is essentially light. The mood of one is the inversion of the mood of the other. In tragedy the hero is defeated by forces outside his control; in comedy the hero overcomes impediments—and usually in an entertaining, humorous way—and is successful. In tragedy man is mastered by fate and nature while in comedy man ludicrously emerges triumphant over opposing forces. While there is thus this basic dichotomy, in both emotion and event, between comedy in its cheerful optimism and tragedy in its somber pessimism, there are nevertheless certain inherent "overlappings" between the two. Most tragedies have a certain amount of humor, often referred to as "comic relief", while most comedies have a certain bitter or serious aspect which is hard to avoid. Shakespeare, in particular, never allows a matter—treated dramatically—to be all funny or all sad. Chekhov always claimed that his play *The Cherry Orchard* was a comedy, while his own director, Stanislavsky, and most audiences have interpreted it as a tragedy. The point is that there are enough similarities of purpose—defining man as both an individual and a member of society—for comedy and tragedy often to work toward similar points. Many plays are simply referred to as "tragic-comedies" because there is such an obvious blend of humor and sadness, lightness and seriousness, concern of the greatest significance and mere frivolity.

Probably the most distinguishing fact of tragedy—conspicuously absent in comedy—is the concept of a hero with some sort of ruinous "flaw". Tragic heroes consistently have some sort of flaw—Othello's pride, Macbeth's ambition, etc. In comedy there is no reason to present some kind of flaw, particularly in the Aristotelian sense, because the hero will be victorious over the forces which oppose him. In tragedy, the hero is an extraordinary figure and usually occupying a high position, whereas the comic hero is not superior to us. Secondly, in tragedy, there are elements of recognition and reversal which lead us to tragic emotions and effects. Thirdly, in comedy, the hero fights against society, not nature or the cosmos. Fourthly, tragedy has grand language, comedy is couched in ordinary expressions.

Roman Drama. As the Roman Republic began to spread in the 4th century BC, it absorbed Greek territories and, naturally,

Greek drama and theatre architecture. Native Roman drama did not develop until the 3rd century BC. Although play production was originally associated with religious festivals, the spiritual nature of the events was soon lost; as the number of festivals increased, drama became primarily a secular entertainment. Not surprisingly, then, the most popular forms were comedy and the native Atellan farce. The great period of Roman playwriting began in the 2nd century BC and was dominated by the comedies of Plautus and Terence, which were adapted from Greek New Comedy. The plays generally involve domestic intrigue, although those of Terence have a moral value as well. Although the plays read much like contemporary comedies, in production one-third to two-thirds of the lines may have been sung.

Although Greek and Roman tragedies were performed during this period, the only extant tragedies, from the 1st century AD, are those of Seneca. They may have been closet dramas—plays written to be recited or simply read and not acted—because by the 1st century AD public interest was too limited to sustain tragedy. Seneca's plays like *Oedipus* and *Phaedra* were based on Greek myths but tended to emphasize supernatural elements, bloody violence, and obsessive passion. The content, form, and devices of Senecan tragedy—a five-act structure that included soliloquies and poetic speeches—became strongly influential in the Renaissance.

The Roman theatre building, as that of Greece, developed after the period of classical writing had ended. In part, this happened because the Romans were afraid to offend one god by building a theatre in honour of another. Only three theatres were constructed in the city of Rome. The use of the arch permitted the construction of free-standing theatre buildings, as opposed to the Greek use of natural slopes and hillsides to support the seating area. Because the chorus had become insignificant, the orchestra was substantially reduced to a small semi-circle. The large stage—about 24 to 30 m (80 to 100 ft) wide—was backed by an elaborate three-story facade with three doors; most Roman comedies are set on a street in front of three houses. As with Greek theatre, scenery was minimal and suggestive.

By the 2nd century AD literary theatre had declined in popularity and was replaced by spectacle and popular entertainment. Even the gladiatorial events were theatricalized with superficial plots, costumes, and settings. Partly because some Roman actors, especially the women, had licentious reputations, and partly because the mimes frequently satirized the Christians, among others, the emerging Christian Church attacked the Roman theatre, thereby contributing to its ultimate demise and to the lingering reputation of theatre and actors as evil or immoral. With the fall of the Roman Empire in AD 476, classical theatre came to an end in the West; mainstream theatrical activity did not re-emerge for more than 500 years. Only the popular entertainers, known as jongleurs and minstrels in the medieval world, survived and provided a thread of continuity. The so-called New Comedy exemplified by Menander was greatly imitated by the Roman comedy writers, in particular by Plautus and Terence in plays like *Eunuchs* and *The Pot of Basil.* Their comedies, in turn, had a great influence on Renaissance and Elizabethan Drama and also on French Neo-classical writer Molière.

Drama in the Middle Ages. Ironically, theatre in the form of liturgical drama was reborn in Europe in the Roman Catholic Church. As the Church sought to extend its influence, it often adopted pagan and folk festivals, many of which had theatrical elements. By the 10th century the various church services provided possibilities for dramatic presentation; indeed, the Mass itself is not unlike a drama. In the late ninth and tenth centuries, there were 'tropes' or musical presentations of certain church services, particularly the various masses. From these musical presentations came drama as the priests began to speak rather than sing the story. So, the 'tropes' represent the beginnings of medieval drama. Eventually, these 'tropes' became independent of the church liturgy and medieval drama was established as a secular entertainment— although religious subjects were still by far the most popular. Gradually, the presentations were moved from the church to the outdoors, particularly into open courtyards. Latin was replaced by the popular vernacular and the audience became more cosmopolitan and representative of larger portions of medieval society. Some of the most popular plays were known as *Mystery Plays*, which were religious plays based on certain events in Biblical history; for the most part, critics have divided the Mystery Plays into three kinds: (i) Old Testament plays, often treating the fall of man, the loss of paradise, etc.; (ii) New Testament plays, usually concerned with the birth of Christ; and (iii) the Death and Resurrection plays. In other words, the story of man and the life and death of Christ became the main subjects of all medieval drama.

As the various kinds of plays were produced with increasing independence from the church, trade guilds toured around the country producing pageants. Another kind of play became popular: scriptural events having to do with miracles and saints. These plays were known as *Miracle Plays* or *Saints' Plays*.

Morality Plays and Interludes. At around the beginning of the fifteenth century emerged the *Morality Play*. It differed from the earlier religious dramas because it contained outright *allegory*: certain abstract passions, vices, and virtues were represented on the stage by actors in bizarre costumes. Thus, the audience could watch such characters as Death, Evil, Mercy, and Shame. Some morality plays deal with a single vice or moral problem, though some deal with the whole moral problem of man's existence. The earliest complete extant morality play is *The Castle of Perseverance* (1425) the theme of which is the fight between mankind's Good Angel and his supporters and his Bad Angel supported by the Seven Deadly Sins. The best known and the most appealing of surviving 15th century morality plays is *Everyman* written in Holland (in Dutch language). The plays, such as *Everyman*, generally dealt with the individual's journey and conduct through life. The allegorical characters include such figures as Death, Gluttony, Good Deeds, and other vices and virtues. The plays are sometimes tedious reading for a modern audience—the rhyme scheme of the verse is often repetitive and sing-song, the plays may be two to three times the length of a Shakespearean drama, and the moral appears obvious and patronizing—but the players interpolated music and action and exploited comic possibilities in many roles of vice figures and Devils to create a popular dramatic form.

The morality plays led slowly to the creation of *interludes* which were relatively short dramas brief enough to be presented in between the other events at feasts, entertainments, etc. The interludes were extremely popular and often consisted of dialogues between only two characters. The interludes sometimes were farces (imitating the French farces) and, in other words, not always serious and religious. Thus, the interlude is often considered to be one of the major secularizing influences on the drama. The whole history of the drama throughout the early and then the late Middle Ages is the gradual evolution of a secular kind of dramatic entertainment. Beginning in church liturgy, drama slowly became liberated from the church and from religious subject matter, and in the Elizabethan era became almost exclusively worldly.

Renaissance Theatre. The Protestant Reformation in northern Europe put an end to most religious drama by the mid-16th century, and a new, dynamic secular drama developed in its place. Although the simple moralities and cycles seem a long way from the dramas of Shakespeare and Molière, the late medieval themes of humankind's struggle and adversity, the turn to secular and temporal concerns, and the reappearance of the comic and grotesque all contributed to the new drama. Moreover, the use of professional players in dramas gradually replaced the use of enthusiastic amateurs.

The Renaissance began at different times in different areas of Europe and was a slow process of change rather than a sudden shift in ideas and values. In theatre, the Renaissance was an attempt to recreate classical drama. Because classical forms and production methods were imperfectly understood, and because the classical ideas were grafted on to contemporary practices and new technologies, Renaissance theatre took on a totally new form with some classical characteristics.

Elizabethan and Jacobean Drama. Renaissance England was sufficiently interested in drama to encourage all sorts of unlikely people from various professions to begin writing plays. By the early seventeenth century, Elizabethan and Jacobean drama had become the best in the history of world literature. How easy it is to mention Shakespeare, but how difficult to mention all of the many others who hardly deserve to be eclipsed by the master—Kyd, Marlowe, Jonson, Beaumont and Fletcher, Ford, Massinger, Marston, Webster, Shirley. The list is endless and the anthologized plays of the Elizabethan and Jacobean theater are more widely read today than the drama of any other period. This is the beginning of new kinds of plays, the romantic comedies, the revenge-murder dramas, the great cycles of history plays, the court comedies, and the pastoral plays. Thus, the Elizabethan stage ushered in an almost unbelievable number of new and talented playwrights, while at the same time it introduced a whole galaxy of new kinds of secular drama, many of which survive to the present day.

After the death of Queen Elizabeth, the drama, reflecting the changing political and social atmosphere, became darker and more sinister in tone, while the comedies, notably those of Jonson, became cynical. An elaborate court theatre, the masque, also developed. Similar to the Italian intermezzi and French ballets, masques presented allegorical stories—often tributes to the royal patron—in dance, music, and spectacle. Jonson was the primary writer of these events, and the architect Inigo Jones frequently designed the fantastic, Italian-style scenery and machinery.

In 1642 civil war erupted, and Parliament, under the influence of the Puritans, closed the theatres until 1660. During that time, most theatre buildings were destroyed and with them most evidence of English Renaissance drama.

Restoration and Eighteenth Century Drama. In the period of the Restoration in England (beginning in 1660 when Charles II was "restored" to the English throne), "heroic plays" became extremely popular. The heroic drama was a kind of tragedy or tragic-comedy characterized by excesses—violence, explosive dialogues, greatly tormented characters, elements of spectacle, and various epic dimensions. The heroic play was almost always located in some distant land, frequently Morocco or Mexico and many other countries. The heroes were usually great military leaders as well as great lovers like Dryden's Antony and consequently often experienced a conflict between their love for a lady and their patriotism. The heroines were almost always virtuous and beautiful, as well as subject to agony over conflicting interests between their hero-lovers and their fathers. Villains were usually power-hungry and villainesses jealous lovers of the heroine's hero! All in all, the plays were easily patterned and some find them too much alike to be individually fascinating. But the heroic drama at least enlarged the dimensions of the world of drama, introduced the bizarre and the fantastic, and created heroes of such stature that their agonies became monstrous and led to great sufferings easily understood by the audience.

During the same period, on the lighter side, the *Comedy of Manners* was born. These plays usually concerned themselves with the manners and customs of a very synthetic or artificial highbrow society; the comedy of manners is a satirical thrust at the mores of the so-called establishment and thus the manners of the upper-crust and the conventions of "social" people are held up for ridicule. Hypocrisy is revealed and absurd incongruities are exposed. Although the tragedies of the period often seem stiff and academic to modern audiences, the witty, sophisticated, sexually suggestive comedies of manners of the period, especially those of William Congreve (like *The Way of the World*), still appeal to many.

Nineteenth Century Drama. The "spectacle" introduced into drama through the heroic plays slowly led into the more extreme spectacle and excessive emotionalism of melodrama in the nineteenth century. Toward the end of the century there was also a revived interest in more serious drama, like that of the Elizabethans, although comedies and tragedies *per se* were not particularly in vogue.

Throughout the 18th century certain philosophical and artistic ideas evolved that eventually coalesced, around the start of the 19th century, into a movement known as Romanticism.

Romantic Theatre. In its purest form, Romanticism concentrated on the spiritual, which would allow humankind to transcend the limitations of the physical world and body and find an ideal truth. Subject matter was drawn from nature and "natural man" (such as the supposedly untouched Native American). Perhaps one of the best examples of Romantic drama is *Faust* (Part I, 1808; Part II, 1832) by the German playwright Johann Wolfgang von Goethe. Based on the classic legend of the man who sells his soul to the devil, this play of epic proportions depicts humankind's attempt to master all knowledge and power in its constant struggle with the universe.

The Romantics focused on emotion rather than rationality, drew their examples from a study of the real world rather than the ideal, and glorified the idea of the artist as a mad genius unfettered by rules. Romanticism thus gave rise to a vast array of dramatic literature and production that was often undisciplined and that often substituted emotional manipulation for substantial ideas.

Romanticism first appeared in Germany, a country with little native theatre other than rustic farces before the 18th century. By the 1820s Romanticism dominated the theatre of most of Europe. Many of the ideas and practices of Romanticism were evident in the late 18th century "Sturm und Drang" movement of Germany led by Goethe and the dramatist Friedrich Schiller. These plays had no single style but were generally strongly emotional, and, in their experimentation with form, laid the groundwork for the rejection of neo-classicism.

The plays of the French playwright René Charles Guilbert de Pixérécourt paved the way for French Romanticism, which had previously been known only in the acting of François Joseph Talma in the first decades of the 19th century. Victor Hugo's *Hernani* (1830) is considered the first French Romantic drama: it broke away from the neo-classical rules.

Melodrama. The same forces that led to Romanticism also led, in combination with various popular forms, to the development of melodrama, the most pervasive dramatic genre of the 19th century. Because it conjures up images of moustache-twirling villains and heroines tied to railway tracks, and because, as literature, it is disdained by most critics, melodrama is generally ridiculed or ignored. Yet it is unquestionably the most popular drama ever produced; it provides a vehicle for spectacular scenic effects and powerful acting; and it furnishes the basis for today's popular theatre—television. The word *melodrama* has two meanings: a mixing of tragedy and comedy (mixed drama), and drama accompanied by music. The latter definition can be applied easily to most film and television production, in which characters are identified by themes, and audience emotions are manipulated through music.

The leading exponent of the form was the German playwright August Friedrich Ferdinand von Kotzebue, the most popular playwright in the world in the 19th century. His more than 200 plays were translated, adapted, or imitated in virtually every Western country. Almost as popular was the prolific French playwright Pixérécourt.

Melodramas are usually in three acts instead of the classical five; plots revolve around the conflict between a virtuous protagonist and an evil villain; the hero overcomes a series of seemingly insurmountable difficulties before triumphing; the plots are often contrived, build to a series of climactic moments, and include many reversals of fate; major events often include such spectacular elements as floods, earthquakes, volcanic eruptions, horse chases, or battles, all graphically depicted onstage. The combination of simple plot, clearly delineated black and white characters, strong emotional values, spectacle, and moral tone made melodrama enormously popular, creating, perhaps, the largest audience in theatre history.

Bourgeois Drama. Through the first quarter of the 19th century, both melodrama and Romanticism tended to be somewhat exotic, focusing on historical or extraordinary events while idealizing or oversimplifying characterization. By the 1830s in England, however, the stylistic elements and characteristics of both turned towards contemporary life and domestic matters and seemingly serious thematic concerns. The plays of writers such as Douglas William Jerrold, Edward Bulwer-Lytton, and later, Dion Boucicault were labelled as domestic melodrama, gentlemanly melodrama, or bourgeois drama. Emphasis was shifted from spectacle and sensation to the recreation of local colour and domestic detail. This required new staging practices that laid the groundwork for much modern stagecraft. The box set came into vogue—a setting depicting three walls of a room with the implication that the audience was observing through an imaginary fourth wall. Three-dimensional furniture replaced the painted representations used previously. Because the sets were no longer mere background, the performers acted as if they were in the real environment of the setting, seemingly unaware of audience's presence. Bits of business developed—instead of assuming a pose and reciting lines, actors created realistic actions, appropriate for the character and situation. More and more attention was paid to accuracy and consistency in costume and setting. Playwrights too paid more attention to realistic detail.

As plays found a larger audience, economic practices altered. Where once actors were part of a repertory company that might perform dozens of plays in continuous rotation over the course of a season, the long run now became more popular. Actors were hired for a single production, to play as many consecutive performances as an audience would pay for.

The Well-made Play. The French equivalent of the bourgeois drama was the so-called well-made play, a form popularized by A. Eugène Scribe and carried on by his follower Victorien Sardou. Similar to melodrama, the well-made play had a highly crafted formula, or structure. The specifics of each play varied, but the structure or plot outline remained basically the same: a careful exposition; a series of incidents leading to a climax; the skilful use of dramatic devices such as reversals, hidden information, important props—a letter, for example, falls into the wrong hands and must be retrieved—and contrived suspense. The well-made-play formula provided the basis for much of later 19th century drama. Alexandre Dumas *fils* and Émile Augier, for example, wrote "thesis plays", which attempted to deal with contemporary social problems.

Naturalism and Social Criticism. By the mid-19th century the interest in realistic detail, psychological motivation for characters, and concern for social problems led to Naturalism in drama. Turning to science for inspiration, the Naturalists felt that the goal of art, like that of science, should be the betterment of life. Dramatists and players should, like scientists, objectively observe and depict the real world. Influenced by the theories of Charles Darwin, the Naturalists believed that heredity and environment are at the root of all human actions and that drama should illustrate this. The Romantic concern for spiritual values was abandoned. The leading Naturalist was the French writer Émile Zola, who compared the playwright to a doctor who must expose disease in order to cure it—the drama therefore had to bring social ills into the open.

The result of this was drama that focused on the seamier elements of society rather than on the beautiful or the ideal. Naturalists sought, in the words of the French playwright Jean Jullien, to present a "slice of life, put on the stage with art". Ideally, a Naturalist play had no beginning, middle, or end or any sort of dramatic contrivance. In practice, of course, incidents were selected and shaped for dramatic effect.

Psychological Realism. Just as drama was moving towards increasing realism in its depiction of the external world, the pioneering 19th century study of psychology led to increasing realism in the psychological motivation of characters. Late 19th century playwrights developed three-dimensional characters placed in realistic settings and situations. The leading playwrights of this style were the Norwegian dramatist Henrik Ibsen and the Swedish author August Strindberg, often considered the founders of modern drama. Their plays deal with such social problems as venereal disease, the sanctity of marriage, and women's rights, but they are also convincingly motivated studies of individuals. In their hands the Naturalistic drama became increasingly introspective. The Irish-born writer George Bernard Shaw was influenced by Ibsen but more in the area of social commentary than in psychological realism.

Nineteenth Century Russian Drama. Russian drama began to develop in the late 18th century. The leading playwrights, such as Alexander Ostrovsky and Nikolay Gogol, were always somewhat realistic in style, but Naturalism became dominant at the end of the 19th century with the plays of Leo Tolstoy and Maxim Gorki. Anton Chekhov has certain Naturalistic characteristics in his writings and was frequently interpreted as a Naturalist. Konstantin Stanislavski, a director who modelled himself at first after the duke of Saxe-Meiningen, founded in 1898 the Moscow Art Theatre with Vladimir Ivanovich Nemirovich-Danchenko for the production of Naturalistic drama. They had particular success with the works of Chekhov. Stanislavski soon realized that real furniture and costumes were insufficient, and that a style of acting was needed that would allow performers to feel and project real emotions. His study led to a system, known as the Stanislavski method, that is still the basis of much actor training today.

Twentieth Century Drama. Many movements, generally lumped together as the avant-garde, attempted to suggest alternatives to the realistic drama and production. The various theoreticians felt that Naturalism presented only superficial and thus limited or surface reality—that a greater truth or reality could be found in the spiritual or the unconscious. Others felt that theatre had lost touch with its origins and had no meaning for modern society other than as a form of entertainment. Paralleling modern art movements, they turned to symbol, abstraction, and ritual in an attempt to revitalize the theatre. Under the leadership of the English drama—particularly the plays of Yeats, Synge, and O'Casey—twentieth century theatre has become vastly popular. We have seen a mushrooming of problem plays and domestic tragedies. For example, it used to be believed that a real 'tragedy' necessarily had to follow the Aristotelian principle that a noble hero suffers a calamitous fall. Now, however, many are quick to grant the status of 'tragic hero' to the pathetic domestic figure of Willy Loman in Arthur Miller's *Death of a Salesman*. T.S. Eliot, Christopher Fry, and Noel Coward are among the many English dramatists who have worked separately for the improvement and advancement of the potentialities of drama. John Osborne's *Look Back in Anger* and Eugene O'Neill's *The Iceman Cometh* exemplify the darkness and anger which have led to a whole new kind of rebellious drama.

The Expressionist movement was popular in the 1910s and 1920s, largely in Germany. It explored the more violent, grotesque aspects of the human psyche, creating a nightmare world onstage. Scenographically, Expressionism is typified by distortion and exaggeration and a suggestive use of light and shadow. The plays, by writers such as Georg Kaiser and Ernst Toller, were episodic and employed staccato—like language and intense imagery. Individualized characters were replaced by stock types or allegorical figures, much as in the morality plays, and plots often revolved around the salvation of humankind. O'Neill was strongly influenced by both Strindberg and the Expressionists; he employed many of their techniques in some of his plays, such as *Emperor Jones* and *Strange Interlude*, to explore the psyches of his characters.

From the time of the Renaissance on, theatre seemed to be striving for total realism, or at least for the illusion of reality. As it reached that goal in the late 19th century, a multifaceted, anti-realistic reaction erupted.

Avant-Garde Precursors of Modern Theatre. Many movements, generally lumped together as the avant-garde, attempted to suggest alternatives to the realistic drama and production. The various theoreticians felt that Naturalism presented only superficial and thus limited or surface reality—that a greater truth or reality could be found in the spiritual or the unconscious. Others felt that theatre had lost touch with its origins and had no meaning for modern society other than as a form of entertainment. Paralleling modern art movements, they turned to symbol, abstraction, and ritual in an attempt to revitalize the theatre. Although realism continues to be dominant in contemporary theatre, its earlier functions are now better served by television and film.

The originator of many anti-realist ideas was the German opera composer Richard Wagner. He believed that the job of the playwright/composer was to create myths. In so doing, Wagner felt, the creator of drama was portraying an ideal world in which the audience shared a communal experience, perhaps as the ancients had done. He sought to depict the "soul state", or inner being, of characters rather than their superficial, realistic aspects. Furthermore, Wagner was unhappy with the lack of unity among the individual arts that constituted the drama. He proposed the *Gesamtkunstwerk*, the "total art work", in which all dramatic elements are unified, preferably under the control of a single artistic creator.

Wagner was also responsible for reforming theatre architecture and dramatic presentation with his Festival Theatre at Bayreuth, Germany, completed in 1876. The stage of this theatre was similar to other 19th century stages even if better equipped, but in the auditorium Wagner removed the boxes and balconies and put in a fan-shaped seating area on a sloped floor, giving an equal view of the stage to all spectators. Just before a performance the auditorium lights dimmed to total darkness—then a radical innovation.

Symbolist Drama. Wagner's ideas were first adopted by the Symbolist movement in France in the 1880s. The Symbolists called for "detheatricalizing" the theatre, meaning stripping away all the technological and scenic encumbrances of the 19th century and replacing them with a spirituality that was to come from the text and the acting. The texts were laden with symbolic imagery not easily construed, rather they were suggestive. The general mood of the plays was slow and dream-like. The intention was to evoke an unconscious response rather than an intellectual one and to depict the non-rational aspects of characters and events. The Symbolist plays of Maurice Maeterlinck of Belgium and Paul Claudel of France, popular in the 1890s and early 20th century, are seldom performed today. Strong Symbolist elements can be found, however, in the plays of Chekhov and the late works of

Ibsen and Strindberg. Symbolist influences are also evident in the works of such later playwrights as the Americans Eugene O'Neill and Tennessee Williams and the Englishman Harold Pinter, propounder of "theatre of silence".

Also influenced by Wagner and the Symbolists were the Swiss scenic theorist Adolphe Appia and the English designer Edward Henry Gordon Craig, whose turn-of-the-century innovations shaped much of 20th century scenic and lighting design. They both reacted against the realistic painted settings of the day, proposing instead suggestive or abstract settings that would create, through light and scenic elements, more of a mood or feeling than an illusion of a real place.

In 1896, a Symbolist theatre in Paris produced Alfred Jarry's *Ubu roi*, for its time a shocking, bizarre play. Modelled vaguely on *Macbeth,* the play depicts puppet-like characters in a world devoid of decency. The play is filled with scatological humour and language. It was perhaps most significant for its shock value and its destruction of virtually all contemporaneous theatrical norms and taboos. *Ubu roi* freed the theatre for exploration in any direction the author wished to go. It also served as the model and inspiration for future avant-garde dramatic movements and the absurdist drama of the 1950s.

Expressionist Drama. The Expressionist movement was popular in the 1910s and 1920s, largely in Germany. It explored the more violent, grotesque aspects of the human psyche, creating a nightmare world onstage. Scenographically, Expressionism is typified by distortion and exaggeration and a suggestive use of light and shadow. The plays, by writers such as Georg Kaiser and Ernst Toller, were episodic and employed staccato-like language and intense imagery. Individualized characters were replaced by stock types or allegorical figures, much as in the morality plays, and plots often revolved around the salvation of humankind. O'Neill was strongly influenced by both Strindberg and the Expressionists; he employed many of their techniques in some of his plays, such as *Emperor Jones* and *Strange Interlude*, to explore the psyches of his characters.

Bertolt Brecht. The German playwright and theoretician Bertolt Brecht also reacted against the realistic drama. Brecht felt that drama could instruct and change society, therefore, it should be political. He believed that effective theatre should bring the audience to the point of decision and action. To accomplish this, he wrote what he called epic—as opposed to dramatic—plays that continuously emphasized the theatrical aspects; the audience was thus constantly reminded that it was in a theatre and could therefore make rational judgements about the material presented. He called this *Verfremdungseffekt* ("alienation effect" or "distancing effect"). The use of a bare stage, exposed lighting and scenic equipment, short scenes, juxtaposition of "reality" with the theatrical presentation—techniques fairly common today—are largely the result of Brecht's influence. Nonetheless, some critics maintain that his most highly regarded plays, e.g. *Mother Courage and Her Children* (1941) and *The Threepenny Opera* (1928, with music by Kurt Weill), do not conform entirely to his theories.

Antonin Artaud. Contemporary with Brecht was the French theoretician Antonin Artaud, whose collection of essays, *The Theatre and Its Double* (1938, trans. 1958), had one of the most profound influences on post-World War II Western theatre. Artaud perceived society as sick and in need of healing. Rejecting psychological drama, he sought instead a religious, communal theatrical experience that would bring about this healing. He compared his concept of "pure" theatre to the plague in its ability to destroy old forms and allow something new and transformed to emerge. Drawing on his imperfect understanding of certain forms of Oriental theatre and primitive ritual, he called for a new language of the theatre, a so-called Theatre of Cruelty. This would jolt spectators by minimizing or eliminating spoken words, using, instead, pure sounds, gestures, and movements and redefining the boundary between actors and spectators. Because Artaud's writings are so ambiguous, and because he provided virtually no concrete examples, his theories gave rise to many, often opposing, forms of theatre.

Absurdist Theatre. The most popular and influential non-realistic genre of the 20th century was absurdism. Spiritually (if not directly) descended from the plays of Jarry, the Dadaists, and the Surrealists, and influenced by the existential theory of Jean-Paul Sartre and the concept of the Absurd of Albert Camus, absurdist dramatists saw, in the words of the Romanian-French playwright Eugène Ionesco, "man as lost in the world, all his actions become senseless, absurd, useless". Best exemplified by Ionesco's *Rhinocéros* (1960) and the Irish-born writer Samuel Beckett's *Waiting for Godot* (1952), absurdist drama tends to eliminate much of the cause-and-effect relationship among incidents, reduce language to a game and minimize its communicative power, reduce characters to archetypes, make place non-specific, and view the world as alienating and incomprehensible.

Absurdism was at its peak in the 1950s, but continued to influence drama through the 1970s. The American playwright Edward Albee's early dramas—*The Zoo Story* and *The American Dream*—were classified as absurd because of the seemingly illogical or irrational elements that defined his characters' world of actions. Pinter was also classed with the absurdists. His plays, such as *The Birthday Party* and *The Homecoming*, seem dark, impenetrable, and absurd. Pinter explained, however, that they are realistic because they resemble the everyday world in which only fragments of unexplained activity and dialogue are seen and heard.

Contemporary Drama. Although pure Naturalism was never very popular after World War I, drama in a realist style continued to dominate the commercial theatre, especially in the United States. Even there, however, psychological realism seemed to be the goal, and non-realistic scenic and dramatic devices were employed to achieve this end. The plays of Arthur Miller and Tennessee Williams, for instance, use memory scenes, dream sequences, purely symbolic characters, projections, and the like. Even O'Neill's later works—ostensibly realistic plays such as *Long Day's Journey into Night* (produced 1956)—incorporate poetic dialogue and a carefully orchestrated background of sounds to soften the hard-edged realism. Scenery was almost always suggestive rather than realistic. European drama was not much influenced by psychological realism but was more concerned with plays of ideas, as evidenced in the works of the Italian dramatist Luigi Pirandello, the French playwrights Jean Anouilh and Jean Giraudoux, and the Belgian playwright Michel de Ghelderode.

In England in the 1950s John Osborne's *Look Back in Anger* (1956) became a rallying point for the post-war "angry young men"; a Vietnam trilogy of the early 1970s, by the American playwright David Rabe, expressed the anger and frustration of many towards the war in Vietnam. Under the influence of Brecht, many post-war German playwrights wrote documentary dramas that, based on historical incidents, explored the moral obligations of individuals to themselves and to society. An example is *The Deputy* (1963), by Rolf Hochhuth, which deals with Pope Pius XII's silence during World War II.

Many playwrights of the 1960s and 1970s—Sam Shepard in the United States, Peter Handke in Austria, Tom Stoppard in England—built plays around language: language as a game, language as sound, language as a barrier, language as a reflection of society. In their plays, dialogue frequently cannot be read simply as a rational exchange of information. Many playwrights also mirrored society's frustration with a seemingly uncontrollable, self-destructive world.

In Europe in the 1970s, new playwriting was largely overshadowed by theatricalist productions, which generally took classical plays and reinterpreted them, often in bold new scenographic spectacles, expressing ideas more through action and the use of space than through language.

In the late 1970s a return to Naturalism in drama paralleled the art movement known as 'Photorealism'. Typified by such plays as *American Buffalo* (1976) by David Mamet, little action occurs, the focus is on mundane characters and events, and the language is fragmentary—much like everyday conversation. The settings are indistinguishable from reality. The intense focus on seemingly meaningless fragments of reality creates an absurdist, nightmarish quality: similar traits can be found in writers such as Stephen Poliakoff. A gritty social realism combined with very dark humour has also been popular; it can be seen in the very different work of Alan Ayckbourn, Mike Leigh, Michael Frayn, Alan Bleasdale, and Dennis Potter.

The History Reviewed. The student should try to remember that drama develops out of the first pagan celebrations of the rites of Dionysius. It follows the original polarization of the emotions into tragedy and comedy but always finds itself forced into hybridized forms. Beginning in around the late fourteenth century, drama begins to become popular through its functional use in the church celebrations of religious events, particularly Easter. Gradually, the religious events become more particular and we discover Miracle plays. Then, with the introduction of allegorical figures onto the stage, we find the morality plays which together with the interludes lead almost directly to the secularized drama of the sixteenth century in England. From the Elizabethan drama to the plays of the present day we discover a continuing revision of both form and subject matter; we have more or less reached the point where almost any subject may be treated dramatically on the stage in whatever ways the playwright chooses. Our understanding of the history of the development of the drama serves as a general background of information on the one hand and as a means of directing attention to the spoken aspect of drama on the other.

THE ORAL NATURE OF DRAMA

It will be clear from our brief survey of the history of drama, and it cannot be too strongly emphasized, that drama is written to be performed. From the early mumblings in Latin to the wild screams of the vernacular, plays have been presented through the medium of the spoken word. We know nothing about the characters except what we are told about them. That is, usually there is no narration or description in drama. Because this is so, the playwright automatically must present his ideas and his pictures of the characters almost entirely through *dialogue* and *action*. Whereas in a novel the author can describe a character fully in an objective way, the only descriptions of a character in a play are those made by other characters—and those descriptions usually must tell us as much about the speaker as about the person to whom that speaker is referring. Thus, when Aristotle described drama as an imitation of an action, he meant the representation or depiction of action through dialogue. Although plays are thus designed to be presented orally on the stage, there is the inescapable fact that at some point the playwright must write down all the words. Eventually, the plays must be read; while Shakespeare's plays were performed before they were read, it has nevertheless been wisely noted that Shakespeare has ultimately had more readers than viewers. As critics of drama attempting to analyze or interpret plays as works of art as well as performances, we must necessarily study the written text. Aristotle's definition of tragedy refers us to the language itself; tragedy, he wrote, is "an imitation of an action of high importance, complete in itself and of some amplitude; in language enhanced by distinct and various beauties, acted not narrated." We can, in other words, study the written language of a play in order to arrive at certain conclusions regarding the play's artistic value. Plays are *literature*, and there is no reason we cannot study them as such, as long as we do not forget that they are written to be acted. For the playwrights have channeled the bulk of his energy and art into the planned *performance* of his play, but in so doing has had to select the right words, images, and sequence of events to make that performance successful. And these may be studied easily through reading the plays.

DRAMATIC CONVENTIONS

Because a play is only—and can only be—an "imitation" or representation of an action, an attempted facsimile of real life, the audience (or reader) must be willing to accept certain things in the imagination. To use Coleridge's famous phrase, the playgoer must be capable of undergoing a "willing suspension of disbelief". That is, if several years pass between one Act and the next while the curtain has been lowered for only ten minutes, the spectator must meet the playwright halfway and accept the passing of time. Just as he must accept the ease with which the location of the play may switch in a matter of seconds from Venice to Cyprus (as in *Othello*) or from Rome to Alexandria (as in *Antony and Cleopatra*). The audience must also accept the fact that when one character "whispers" to another, it must be loud enough for every one in the theatre to hear; while it should also be noted that so-called "asides" which the other characters are not supposed to hear are obviously delivered in loud enough voices for them to hear. While these conventions may seem too obvious to need discussion, they should be kept in mind if only to help the students to visualize mentally the way a play "works" when performed on stage. Within every play, action, place and time must be accepted as the playwright urges or else the play may become meaningless; and at the same time that these general conventions hold true for all drama, the students should slowly familiarize themselves with the lesser conventions of particular kinds of plays.

REALISM AND DEPARTURE FROM IT

Every critic of drama must determine whether a particular playwright is attempting to show certain characters as examples of the way people "really are" or whether, on the contrary, the playwright is merely presenting them in dramatic entertaining ways, making them larger than real life people in order to crystallize certain truths about man and the human predicament. At certain points in the history of the drama, dramatists have offered to the audience characters essentially unreal or contrived, while others in earnest attempted to hold up a mirror to society. In any case, the students should understand clearly which approach to reality the dramatist has taken, for this approach will determine the conventions which he will use as well as his methods of characterization.

2

Defining a Play

Introduction. As there are so many different kinds of drama, it is only logical that the students begin their analysis of a play with an extended definition. This does not simply mean to say that the students should understand that the play is a comedy or a tragedy, but rather that the students attempt to delineate accurately the "particular world" of this particular play. We should try to think of all of the dimensions of any drama and then briefly describe the way these dimensions are discovered in a particular play. In this way, we automatically suggest the ways in which a particular play is "conventional" and the ways in which it is "peculiar" or "unique".

DESCRIBING THE WORLD OF THE DRAMA

This is perhaps the most essential task of the students: to analyze, explain and describe the world of the play. For example, let us imagine that we want to write a paper on *Macbeth*. Our first job is to suggest the entire mad world of the play, the Halloween-type modulations, the witches dancing around the boiling cauldron, Lady Macbeth wringing her hands. We want to suggest—or even evoke—the entire macabre world in which Shakespeare's characters move in this particular play. Let us take another example this time from modern drama. Consider Arthur Miller's Pulitzer Prize-winning play, *Death of a Salesman*. We could begin our definition of the play in the following manner—this is a dark play which graphically illustrates the frustration, despair of an unsuccessful human being. From beginning to end, Miller takes the audience into a very somber world where humour itself somehow only serves to underline the futility of certain kind of existence. The main character, Willy Loman, goes on an interior journey; he has no real past or future but instead he carries both in his yet "realistic" present. His surroundings blend into those of his past while they flirt with those of his future, and the result is a world of timelessness. As Willy Loman relives his life constantly, he almost ceases to live at all, and his final suicide only magnifies the kind of lifeless world in which he has lived. His world is filled with death, and this is the world of the drama as a whole. There are many hopeful alternatives to Willy Loman's tragedy but at the same time there is macabre inevitability working in the world of the play, an inevitability of death which Miller reinforces and impresses upon the audience at all times. The world of the play is dark and dreary; there is much anxiety and little hope, much labour and little peace, strained human relationships and denuded unattractive human emotions like lust and hate. Miller has presented a world purposefully morose and unsatisfying—and at the same time very meaningful.

The Kind of Play. One has to recognize the importance of "placing" a play in the generic sense. We have seen in the Introduction there is a wide variety or kinds of plays, ranging from the Miracle play of the late fifteenth century to the Restoration Comedy. Thus, it is important to explain in the beginning of any analysis and interpretation that the play does belong to the type known as.... Then students may even want to note that the play accordingly makes use of certain conventions common to this kind of play, i.e. if the play is a 'heroic drama' a student can notice that the hero is typically a great warrior and lover, and like so many heroes of heroic plays is torn between duty and love. In other words, the process of defining a play—this is how analysis and interpretation of every play should begin—is largely helped by reference to the kind of play and the conventions of that kind of play. If one wants to speak about a "tragic hero", to remind the readers what the Aristotelian criteria for the tragic hero were, then suggest whether or not the hero in question fulfills those criteria. We can, in other words, point out the expected conventions of the kind of the play and the extent to which the playwright makes use of them.

THE PHYSICAL WORLD OF THE PLAY

It would be futile to enter immediately in to a discussion of the play without some brief explanation of the physical world in which it takes place. This means, first of all, explaining the "location". Where does the action take place? Do we move from one part of the world to another as in *Antony and Cleopatra* or do we stay in one home almost the whole time as in *All My Sons*? If the location has some symbolic or historical significance, this should be explained at the outset. For example, much of the action of *Othello* takes place in Cyprus while some of it takes place in Venice; the critic would have to explain that Cyprus belonged to the Venetian State and that it was threatened, then finally conquered by the enemy Turks and made a part of the Turkish empire. Our understanding of the play can never be complete without at least this sort of minimal reference to the location. Furthermore, by the "physical world of the play" we also denote the time of the day. What is the length of the play? Are there intervals of time between scenes? Acts? Does the whole take place in the classically specified time of twenty-four hour?

By placing the play in time and space we are clarifying the larger world with which the playwright is concerned, the world of action and character. But how futile it is to begin with only what is major without illuminating what is minor. If we did not comment on the location of the play and the passage of time, we would assume too much in our audience. Thus, the students should always begin with the essential attributes of the play's physical location in time and space.

The Central Theme. Every play presents one or many ideas which we call the "theme". This is the ultimate significance of any play and one dimension of the artist's labour which outlives entertainment value. What, we always ask, does the play "mean"? If we are going to discuss Miller's *Death of a Salesman*, to continue with the example used earlier, we need to state that the theme is the futility of rationalization in the face of death. Willy Loman's tragic flaw is pride; the theme is thus, in the final sense, how pride leads to destruction and death. Pride is valueless in a certain context. Miller realized that he was taking a domestic, bourgeois character for a tragic hero but also realized that pride had interfered with his whole life; if the hero could remember his life and his disappointments, he could not help but be driven to ultimate suicide. The theme of pride leading to destruction determined in a great way the actual final structure of the play. Thus, the theme (the basic idea) of the play largely determined the execution of the play. The students, thus, should state the theme as best they can in the very beginning of their definition of the play.

Part of our process of defining the play is our early suggestion of the meaning of the play. We address ourselves immediately to what the play is about, for it would be pointless to describe the physical world, the location, time, setting, dominant atmosphere or emotional framework, without at least the suggestion of meaning. However, most of our comments on the meaning of the play should be held back until later in our analysis. The meaning is, ultimately, our major concern and thus the concern we want to work up to rather than begin with. It is enough to suggest that a play is, say, about death caused by pride; it is not necessary to explore all the dimensions of the theme and the various implications of the action until the major groundwork has been presented, the major theme, its importance, its centrality, and its execution are thus only presented in a "general" way, thereby forming part of our opening set of definitions of the play's world. For every play is located not only in space and in time but in the imagination and intellect as well. For example, if the playwright is urging the audience towards a particular kind of moral action, we need to define it before we can adequately grasp the significance of the actions of the characters.

Characters Defined. Part of any first general definition of a drama should refer to the major characters in a literal and informative manner, i.e. we should briefly note that the play has a certain number of characters, that only four, for example, are "major" characters while the others are "minor" ones, and then we should present brief descriptions of each of them. For example, in our general definition of *Othello* we would need to note that the play is about the slow development of the jealousy of the Moor Othello. Then we would correctly point out that Othello is one of the two major male characters, the other being Iago, and that there are two other major male characters of somewhat less importance, Cassio and Roderigo. Then we would note that on the distaff side we have only Desdemona to contend with, that she is the new bride of Othello, and that her serving woman is Emilia, the coarse wife of Iago. In short, we would present a quick run down of the characters involved in one way or another in most of the play's action. We would hardly define a play in any real way without at least suggesting some of the character relationships.

Plot. We should discuss the organisation of the major action of the drama in question so that the characters' relationships will become clarified with reference to the main events of the play. We need to make some sort of correlation between the action and the theme: how does the action translate into meaning? Why are certain events more important than others? What is the principal event (or action) in the play? Our definition of the play is more or less completed by our brief discussion of what actually happens in a general way. We need not make a full-scale investigation into the subtleties of structure or the motivations of the various characters, but we need to present a synopsis of the main action.

Sources. A less significant but nevertheless essential part of any opening definition of a drama is one of reference to the source of the drama, i.e. we should at least insert parenthetically or in apposition the place where the play story was probably discovered. Obviously, this does not hold true when dealing with many modern plays, but most plays of the Elizabethan stage and many of those of the Restoration are indebted to stories told elsewhere by other authors.

Prose and Verse Style. A definition should include at least some mention, however brief, of the basic style of the play. For example, if we were discussing Shakespeare's *A Midsummer Night's Dream* we might notice in our definition that a large part of the characterization is accomplished through stylistic changes: that Theseus and Hyppolyta speak a high-blown regal language while Bottom and his company speak a very ordinary low one, and that even the language of Pyramus and Thisbe in the "play within a play" is of a humorously absurd ballad meter. When we think of style we must of course try to think quickly of all the various considerations which come under the general category of style, such as diction, the use of figurative language, patterns of imagery, rhetorical devices, emphasis, and even logic. If there is some outstanding characteristic of the style—such as the heavy use of the allegory or irony—this should be noted in the opening definition. And the students should attempt to make some sort of general statement as to whether the play is written in "ornate" or "plain" style, as well as whether the dialogue is mostly in the "vernacular" or is "formal", is "rhymed" or "unrhymed". Only the basic skeleton of the stylistic particularities need to be noted, for they will suffice for purposes of definition.

Outstanding Feature of the Play. If there is some one aspect of the entire play, in either construction, meaning, or style, it should be separately noticed and emphasized accordingly. In many plays no one aspect will be so dominant that it needs to be especially noticed; sometimes, however, as with O'Neill's *The Iceman Cometh*, there is one exceptional fact about the play, in this case it runs some six hours when performed, or several hours longer than most plays. O'Neill actually experimented with writing several very long plays and this is one of the outstanding facts about those plays. Shakespeare's *Twelfth Night* derives almost all of its energy, plot, story, etc. from the one outstanding theatrical "device" or "convention" of "mixed identity". *Othello* is one of the few plays to depend so thoroughly on a single "gimmick", Desdemona's handkerchief, which keeps changing hands in the play. Milton's *Samson Agonistes* is the first classical Greek tragedy written in English and not to mention this would be a severe example of "conspicuous omission". Ben Jonson's *Every Man in His Humour* has at its centre a newly revived psychology of humours and the play would at best be only partly understood aside from this theory. In Bertolt Brecht's *The Good Woman of Setzuan* several characters come centre-stage and suddenly interrupt the entire action by singing songs. This is one of the outstanding aspects of this Brecht play and of other Brecht plays; the student needs to refer to the singing and then to Brecht's strongly believed theory that when a song is being sung in a play it should stand out and not be incorporated into the main action of the play. Brecht believes in calling a spade a spade (to echo Dr. Samuel Johnson) and thus a song is a song and should be presented as such. In other words, whenever there is any aspect of a play which is conspicuous in some sense, it should be highlighted as a part of the definition.

EXAMPLES OF DEFINING THE DRAMA

Othello. Shakespeare's *Othello*, a tragedy written in his middle period after *Hamlet*, is a play about jealousy and, in particular, about the way in which a sinister villain, Iago, makes the General Othello believe that his wife, Desdemona, is having an illicit affair with his lieutenant, Cassio. The world of the play is physically located in Venice and Cyprus. Othello is sent by the senate of Venice to defend Cyprus against an expected invasion by the enemy Turks. Historically, toward the end of the sixteenth century Cyprus was in fact so invaded and passed from the ownership of Venice into the growing Turkish empire.

The play's action covers several days all together and events follow upon one another in extremely rapid succession. Iago's increasing ability and success in duping the rather naïve and jealous Othello becomes rather gruesome to observe, as does the futility of Desdemona's purity and innocence. The play works through the development of Othello's jealousy into a kind of animalistic madness which leads him to murder Desdemona and then, when learning of his wrong murder, to commit suicide. The action relates carefully to the theme, for as the play progresses we see the increasing malignity of the monstrous emotion, jealousy. In Shakespeare's source, a tale from the collection of tales—*Heccatommithi*—written by the Italian novelist Giraldi Cinthio, Iago has a considerable love for Desdemona, which thus constitutes his major motivation for hurting Othello. But Shakespeare has transformed Iago into something of an evil figure, a character who embodies all the force of evil.

Othello is written in a style based on characterization. Othello himself speaks as military man, a "doer" rather than a thinker, while Iago speaks in the language of craft and cunning. There are various patterns of imagery in the play, as we shall see in the further analysis, and all of them help us to understand basic difference between the two central characters, Iago and Othello. The outstanding feature of the development of play's story is the use of the theatrical device of the handkerchief—which Othello gives to Desdemona, which Desdemona drops, which Emilia finds and gives to Iago, which Iago drops on the floor in Cassio's room, which Cassio finds, which Cassio gives to Bianca, etc. The whole play, in a certain sense, is about a handkerchief, as we watch the handkerchief frequently change hands we are led into an increased awareness of the logical development of Othello's unfounded jealousy. With these brief sketches of the world of the play, the characters, the action, the style, and some of the usual facts about the play, such as Shakespeare's modification of his sources and his use of the devise of the handkerchief, let us turn our attention to the analysis and interpretation of the play's central meaning and all of its implications, particularly as they arise from the patterns of imagery.

The Iceman Cometh. The key development of this play is the way in which the audience is only slowly led to understand Hickey's insanity; the world of pipedreams inhabited by all of the characters is stark and barren. There is little relief and the play is designed to last about six hours. O'Neill is taking the audience on a very long, close-up tour of "the other half" and it is easy to understand their creations of false hopes and faith in better "tomorrows". Against false dreams Hickey keeps placing self-knowledge. The surprise of the play is the depiction of Hickey's own acquisition of self-knowledge which has culminated in his self-admission of his attitude towards his wife and her relations with the iceman. Toward the end of the play the truth about Hickey is revealed. The jokes about how "the iceman cometh" acquire a firm symbolism in an equation between the figurative iceman and death. Death comes to everyman after a certain number of "tomorrows" after their pipedreams have passed away.

While the play is about death, and while the play presents a basically depressing group of characters, O'Neill understands that life—even in its darkest aspects—is not without some humour and thus there is certain amount of light comic-relief throughout the play, particularly in the early characterization of Hickey and in the comments which some of the others make about him.

The prose style of the play is extremely lowbrow; the language spoken is all in the dialogue of the vernacular, the tough West side New York accent with the butchered syllables and "dem" for "them". O'Neill successfully captures the human spirit of a collection of degenerates on a hot summer day in a bar in New York. We can define the play as a tour of the dark side of humanity, the social slums created and sustained by unrealistic dreams and rationalizations. O'Neill holds up nothing back in the gradual introduction of death, taking us thus to the inevitable conclusion of despair. By subjecting the audience to a six-hour close-up view of a horrible reality, O'Neill automatically creates empathy and forces us toward re-evaluation and self-acknowledgement. The play is defined in stark terms; we need little embellishment to grasp the central aspect of the play—death—in all its reality. We need little imagination to enter into the private rationalization, guilt, and despair of the suffering hardware salesman Hickey. O'Neill has carefully constructed his plot so that he can preserve the unities of space and time, and in doing so he has written a masterful study of human despair in the extreme, where cowardly survival is only a hair's breadth away from courageous defeat.

DEFINITION AS A PRELUDE TO ANALYSIS/INTERPRETATION

The definition of a play may or may not be included as a formal part of a paper, i.e. the student should write out some kind of defining comments like those we have presented for *Othello* and *The Iceman Cometh*, but at the same time it is important to realize that these defining remarks do not necessarily have to be incorporated into an analytical paper. In general some sort of definition is the best way to enter a play and begin discussion on a more advanced level. The definitions will be helpful whether or not they are used formally in the paper, for the first definition of the play is really the prelude to further analysis and interpretation of the various aspects of the play—characters, plot, structure, meaning, style, etc. It is not difficult to see that if the student were to begin with a complicated kind of analysis, he would be beginning 'in media res' (in the middle of things) and thus would not necessarily win the reader's attention. Furthermore, most college teachers of composition emphasize the importance of definition in both thinking and papers. By presenting a general description of the play, by defining it as a comedy or tragedy, by noting the characters and the general course of the action, the student eases himself and the reader into a more receptive mood; thus the definition should be seen as a prelude, a preliminary requirement, to more advanced analysis. And the whole process of defining should be maintained throughout the analysis. If we begin to speak of the major character as a "tragic hero" we should define precisely what we mean by "tragic hero". In other words, by defining the play before analyzing particular aspects of it, the student introduces the paper, in a relaxed and interesting way while reminding himself of the importance of creating and maintaining definitions throughout the analysis.

3

Dramatic Structure

The word 'structure' refers to the total organization of a literary work. When we delineate the structure we are, in effect, making the summary of the full scheme or plan of the work. In essence, analysis and interpretation of structure is twofold; we begin by outlining the way in which the play is put together, and then suggest reasons 'why' the playwright chose a particular way of assembling the events of the play. Finally, we evaluate the structure with regard to its apparent effectiveness.

CLASSICAL TRAGIC STRUCTURE

One of the most dominating theories of structure is that which classically pertained to tragedies. Because a tragedy deals with conflict, ancient critics thought of the plays as tying and untying knots. Most of the efforts of the play will go into the "tying" aspect, for we usually work up toward a knot (catastrophe) for a considerably longer time, than we work down from it. In any case, the view of tragedy has frequently and consistently taken a dividing approach which separates the events of the play into four larger categories: (i) rising action, (ii) climax (turning point), (iii) falling action, and (iv) catastrophe.

Rising Action. Rising action is the entire first part of the play in which the forces creating conflict are delineated, enlarged, and prepared for some disaster. Preceding the rising action there is often what we simply call "introduction" or "exposition", a short section directly in the beginning in which we are made acquainted with certain facts, usually pertaining to events which have occurred before the beginning of the time of the play. We speak generally then of the exciting action, i.e. the few events or ideas which excite the play into motion. For example, a certain character is stirred up when he hears a report that his close friend or relative has been murdered. When such a character vows revenge we have reached a major turning point in the play, the climax, for the forces enraging the hero have led him into a decision to further action, action out of the ordinary, etc. The rising action is generally similar to a building wave which we know will reach a peak and prepare to crash on shore. It usually carries the hero through a series of events which enlarge and intensify his conflict. We often find ourselves wondering how long the hero will be able to endure his oppression before he decides to retaliate in one way or another. The competing forces become more and more antagonistic and we sense that the hero is caught or being crushed between them.

Climax. The first pause in the play occurs when the hero makes a decision or makes some all-important "discovery" about either himself or someone else in the play, the act which interrupts everything else that is happening, is always referred to as the climax. This is the end of the rising action, for it constitutes a major turning point in the play. We are now moving suddenly in a very different direction, often because the hero has some new knowledge or determination.

Falling Action. The falling action follows the climax and usually presents the ways in which the hero is slowly overpowered and becomes increasingly helpless. We see him as representative of man bound up in a fate which he is powerless to master. The falling action does not usually last as long as the rising action. Because there is inevitably such intense emotionalism in the falling action, the playwright often provides comic-relief.

Catastrophe. The catastrophe is the main action of the play and is often a death, usually the death of the hero or the heroine (or both, as in *Othello*). The catastrophe is the one event in the play toward which everything else has been working, either directly or indirectly. The catastrophe, though depressing and usually unpleasant, satisfies because it fulfills the audience's expectations. The catastrophe is almost always the logical result of the rising and falling action; the catastrophe is the death which the audience has expected for a long time. Sometimes there is a final pause of suspense in which it appears momentarily that the final death will not arrive, but then the death does arrive, and the pause has rendered it both exciting and logical. Often there is a very short detailed section of the play following the catastrophe. The playwright merely pulls together the few loose threads of the story so that the audience understands what will become of the surviving characters.

The five-part dramatic structure of exposition, rising action, climax, falling action, and catastrophe rarely coincides with the five acts of most plays. Often the climax, for example, does not arrive until the fourth act, while the exposition rarely takes up more time than the first scene and almost never occupies us for the entire first act. (But it should be noted that in Ibsen and Chekhov, the exposition is spread over several acts.) In any case, most plays—and not only tragedies—have the integral parts which we have outlined. This can well be seen if we consider some examples, dividing the actions of well-made plays into the conventional categories.

STRUCTURE: EXAMPLES

Death of a Salesman. If we wanted to divide the play according to traditional categories, we would do it in the following way: the rising action would describe all of the opening false optimism of Willy Loman, his pride in his two sons, his feeling of superiority over his neighbour, his hopes for the future. The climax would arrive when the audience hears the way in which Biff Loman discovered his father Willy in a compromising situation. This discovery had been the ruining factor of Biff's entire life. Once he realized that his father was a hypocrite and a lecherous unfaithful husband, he was no longer able to function as he had in the past. This discovery of his father's affair is the climax in the sense that it ruins the chances for any success in a father-son relationship, the relationship which had been hoped for in the beginning of the play. The falling action would include Willy's feelings of sinking deeper and deeper. He realizes that his sons are doomed to be failure like himself and that it is his own fault that they will fail, particularly because of the way in which his behaviour led to Biff's loss of respect. Thus, Willy is in debt, in total despair, and this leads to the final catastrophe of the play. The last few minutes of the play present Happy optimistically vowing to continue in his father's footsteps. We sense the irony here, for we know that Happy, like his father, will be a failure, will be crushed by forces which he cannot control.

While we can thus enhance our grasp and understanding of Miller's play by reviewing the action in terms of rise and fall, we need to isolate those aspects of this particular play which make its structure unusual. We need to be able to understand structure not only in the conventional way but in the exceptional ways as well. Thus, in this particular play the structure is determined—as Miller has himself explained—by the way in which Willy Loman thinks at this particular moment in his life. The locale shifts from the present to the past as Willy imagines the glorious deeds of the past. Furthermore, Willy's despair over the father-son relationship is clear from the very beginning of the play. When we meet Willy Loman we know that he is a doomed man; thus even though we are "left in" on certain facts—such as the climactic destructive discovery of Willy's adultery—we always know where we are going, and perhaps this is explained by the fact that the only thing Miller knew when he sat down to write the play was that Willy was going to die. The structure of the play is thus to some extent almost predetermined, evolving naturally from Willy's manner of thinking. The play mingles the past with the present because this is the way Willy thinks; the play moves in imagination and yet maintains unity of place; the entire structure is thus determined by the playwright's understanding of his hero, while at the same time it can be understood in the conventional terms of tragic structure.

Dr. Faustus. Marlowe's famous play (probably completed in the winter of 1588-89) is often cited as an example of Elizabethan tragedy at its best. But the play interests us at the moment because although it can be divided in the usual way, it can more readily be divided in a different way. The point is that while we want always to use our major categories when we first start thinking about the structure of any play, we want further to make our final comments dependent on the particular distinction of structure in the play which we are examining.

Thus, let us begin briefly by considering the play's action in the conventional manner. The story of *Dr. Faustus* is very well-known and has been used in the twentieth century by the novelist Thomas Mann. In Marlowe's play, we first hear from the chorus, which quickly tells us of Faustus' early life; all of this is the basic "introduction" in the play. The rising action covers Faustus' conversations with the Good Angel and the Bad Angel (in their opposition is the conflict of Faustus himself) and the appearance of the devil Mephistopheles—who humorously notes that he always appears when someone is dissatisfied and angry with God. In any case, the climax arrives—the turning point of the play—when Faustus signs a pledge in blood that he will give his soul to the devil in return for twenty-four years of supernatural power. The falling action covers Faustus' various diversions while using his new evil powers, such as when he makes himself invisible and goes to Rome, where he pesters the Pope. It is falling action because we know that Faustus' life is growing short, that he is bound on a one-way trip to his eventual arrival in hell. At the end we find the expected catastrophe—the death of Faustus, his going to hell, and the tearing off of all his limbs by the devils as he dies. Thus, the *Tragical History of Doctor Faustus* can be understood structurally in the conventional ways. But in what other ways can we divide the play? What is particular about the structure of Marlowe's play?

In the first place, the surviving text of the play has no formal division into acts or scenes, although the material is easily arranged into five acts. And while we can talk about the play in the standard manner, it seems better to divide the play simply into three parts: (i) that which pertains to the creation of the bond between Faustus and Mephistopheles; (ii) Faustus' enjoyment of his new powers; (iii) the fulfillment of the bond, that is Faustus' death. This is the easiest way to discuss the structure of the play in a broad sense but should not be considered as incompatible with our first manner of discussing the structure. Both the five part and the three part division of the play explain the events in terms of the exposition, rising action, climax, falling action, and expected catastrophe.

Marlowe's play has certain structural facets which need mentioning. As with *Death of a Salesman*, Marlowe's *Dr. Faustus* plays tricks with time. We are witnessing, we should remember, the passage of twenty-four years in just a few hours. Marlowe achieves this effect by using numerous short scenes, often transporting Faustus to some faraway place (such as his glimpse of hell). This passage of so much time makes the play automatically very different from the Classical Greek tragedy, which (generally) takes place within twenty-four hours. And, finally, like so many Shakespearean tragedies, Marlowe's play contains a good deal of comedy which is very entertaining, particularly the scene preceding the signing of the bond in which Marlowe delivers a wonderful comic irony by having Wagner and the clown saying that they would not give their soul to the devil even for a leg of mutton.

Antigone. *Antigone* is one of the seven surviving plays out of over a hundred written by the famous Greek tragedian Sophocles (495-405 B.C). It is in all respects a "representative" Greek tragedy and along with *Oedipus the King* is widely read and praised. Like so many Greek tragedies, *Antigone* deals with the way in which a noble man brings death upon his family because of his own tragic flaw of pride. Our immediate concern is with the structure of the play: how is the action to be divided?

The exposition arrives in the opening prologue in which we learn that the new king Creon of Thebes has declared that the body of Polyneices is not to be buried but instead allowed to lie in the open and rot. Polyneices' brother Eteocles has died defending his country and thus has been honorably buried while Polyneices has broken the terms of his banishment and died for no good cause. Antigone, sister to these brothers, wants to give Polyneices a decent burial and tries to enlist the aid of her sister Ismene. Ismene, however, refuses. This then is the opening information of the play; we learn of the general problem at the outset. This problem becomes more complicated as the story develops. In the rising action Antigone makes an attempt to sneak out to the body of Polyneices to clean it and bury it in an honourable way. Creon, meanwhile, makes a public proclamation of his desire that the body not be touched by anyone. We immediately have two contrasting views of the dead body and thus a real conflict. The climax arrives when a report comes that the body of Polyneices has in fact been buried. Creon's pride will have been thus directly challenged; the two sides in conflict have declared an open war; the announcement of the burial of Polyneices is thus the major turning point in the play.

The falling action, leading to disaster, involves a series of events—Creon's sentencing of Antigone to a slow death in a vault in the desert; Creon's accusal of Ismene as an accomplice of Antigone; Creon's fight with his son Haimon, who predicts that when Antigone dies someone else will die, Tiresias' predictions of disaster, and finally the resulting attempt by Creon at the last minute to change his former decree. But the audience well knows that Creon has waited too long, that he has been too proud, and that his pride will lead to disaster.

The catastrophe arrives as expected in the form of death (the usual form of the catastrophe in tragedy, and particularly in Greek tragedy). First, there is the reference to the death of Antigone, who has hung herself. Then we hear how Haimon thrusts first at his father Creon, but missing him, immediately kills himself. When Creon returns to the city of Thebes carrying in his arms his dead son, he is warned that still more grief awaits him, then hears that his wife Eurydice has stabbed herself and died cursing Creon. Thus, the catastrophe is a series of three unsuccessful deaths all indirectly caused by the pride and stubbornness of Creon. Thus, the play moves in fairly rapid succession through a series of events all relating to the opening problem of the disposal of the slain corpse of Polyneices. That arguments over death lead to death is of course a kind of poetic justice, as it were, while Sophocles adheres rigidly to the demands of formal classical tragic structure. The exposition, rising action, climax, falling action, and catastrophe all lead logically and smoothly into the multiple deaths in the end of the play. The last small pause arrives when the chorus steps forward (as Creon enters his house) and announces the moral of the play: that there can be no happiness where there is no wisdom, and that proud men eventually learn in their old age how to be wise—only after their lack of wisdom has brought them great misery.

In contrast with Marlowe's *Dr. Faustus* and Miller's *Death of a Salesman*, there is no real reason to discuss the structure of *Antigone* in any other way, for it makes such good sense when discussed in the classical manner. One of the true aspects of the genius of Sophoclean tragedy is that the structure is very aptly designed. All of the small incidents follow the established conventions of the day—for example, we do not see the deaths on the stage but instead only hear about them through reports. Part of the play's structure is thus designed to accommodate this kind of convention; the fact that Polyneices' corpse has been buried must be reported just as Creon must be told that Eurydice has slain herself. The real conflict of the play is as usual that between the will of a proud man and the will of the gods and Antigone, who obeys it. Creon only slowly realizes that he, and not the gods, must yield. Throughout the play Creon openly defies the gods and and he is justly punished by them. The structure is designed to work through the creation, enlargement, and resolution of this central conflict in a logical and dramatic way; thus the structure expertly serves thematic needs.

Othello. Shakespeare's *Othello* provides a useful plot for division into exposition, exciting action, rising action, climax, falling action, and catastrophe. The introduction informs us that Desdemona, the daughter of a Venetian nobleman, Brabantio, has eloped with the black moor Othello. The exciting action is Iago's resentment that Othello has promoted the Florentine Michael Cassio to the position of lieutenant instead of Iago himself; this resentment excites Iago into a decision to work for the downfall of both Cassio and Othello. The rising action is the series of ways in which Iago works to make Othello begin to have suspicions of his wife's having a secret romance with Cassio. The turning point or climax of the play is when Othello believes that he overhears Cassio talking lewdly about Desdemona (Cassio is talking about his mistress Bianca). The falling action constitutes Othello's increasing madness and jealousy and his plots to kill Cassio and Desdemona. The catastrophe arrives when he murders the innocent Desdemona and then, after learning that he has been tricked by Iago, stabs himself. As usual, the tragedy has moved swiftly toward a resolution of conflict through sorrowful death.

Othello, like *Antigone*, thus employs the kind of logical structure necessary to develop the events of the story in a logical and exciting way. However, often a dramatist is unable to use the so-called classical system of tragedy and must present his story in some other way. This leads to a brief mention of other kinds of plot.

PLOT

Plot is the central aspect of all drama, for drama is primarily concerned with "what happens". "Plot" is basically another term for structure, the difference being that when we discuss plot we are more or less committed to discuss everything that happens in the play. A play is composed of a series of incidents or episodes which follow after one another according to some plan of the playwright; every incident is connected—often in a subtle way—to incidents which follow. Antigone could not bury the body of Polyneices if his body were not lying out on the desert in the open any more than Creon could sentence Antigone to death if she had not committed a crime and acted against the will of the state as represented in Creon. In other words, when we talk about plot we are talking about all of the various incidents in the play (and by definition no plot can exist with only one incident), and the ways in which those incidents connect. Most plays are said to have a beginning, a middle, and an end, while within each of three sections (how aptly this fits Marlowe's *Dr. Faustus*) there are varying number of small incidents.

Any plot of a dramatic work necessarily has to do with conflict. Throughout the play there are repeated challenges of one force by another; Antigone clashes with the gods, Faustus tries to sell his soul to his advantage. A plot presents incidents in which the opposing forces meet head-on until there is some sort of final resolution (catastrophe). Perhaps the most important aspect of plot is its relationship to character. Everything in the plot—i.e. every incident—is introduced because of the particular feelings of a particular character at a particular time. There is nothing in the play which is not a product of character motivation. What plot does, then, is translate the essence of the characters' ideas into appropriate actions. Plot informs us as to what the characters are like. Thus, while we talk about the structure of a play in terms of artistic development and relationship of parts, we also need to refer specifically to the plot, to the actions which, in effect, delineate the characters. All of the actions arise out of the characters and thus we must explain the actions in terms of the characters— Antigone buries Polyneices because she wants to honour her brother; Roderigo agrees to aid Iago in his plans against Othello and Cassio because he wants a chance for himself to win Desdemona; Willy Loman commits suicide because he is no longer able to cope with an oppressive world. When we discuss plot then, no matter for what ultimate purpose, we necessarily need to pay more attention to the fine points regarding the various characters.

HISTORICAL CHANGES IN STRUCTURE

In the nineteenth century, largely because of the influence of Ibsen, drama ceased to adhere to any formal presentation of rising action, climax, falling action, and catastrophe, however, almost all plays still contain theses various stages of development, the main difference being that in some plays parts of the structural development are presented to the audience by way of "flashback" and in general may follow a less rigid time scheme. Even Miller's *Death of a Salesman*, however, as we have seen, relies on rising action, climax, etc. even though much of it is developed through dreaming back into the past in the mind of Willy Loman. If a play thus opens closer to the actual catastrophe than originally, the events leading to the catastrophe are nevertheless introduced, even if indirectly. Thus, the basic dramatic structure—in its essence—is virtually static and timeless. There is almost no play that cannot be discussed in terms of exposition, exciting action, rising action, climax, falling action, and catastrophe, and thus the student would do well to begin every consideration of style in this time-tested way, then begin to look for unusual aspects of the play's structure, such as the long span of time covered in Marlowe's *Dr. Faustus*.

THE RARE STRUCTURE

Riders to the Sea. Not every play can be discussed both in terms of rising action and climax, etc. as well as in terms of peculiarities of structure. Many plays are simply constructed in an entirely individual way and any analysis of structure needs to focus on this individuality. An example of this kind of play is John Synge's short play *Riders to the Sea*. There are no acts or scene divisions. There are no incidents as such, but only reports of incidents. It is possible for a single location to refer obliquely and directly to other locations—as we saw in Miller's *Death of a Salesman*—and this is the case in Synge's famous short play.

The plot—what happens—is not particularly complicated. Cathleen and Nora, two daughters of an old woman named Maurya are talking in the kitchen of their small cottage on an island off the west of Ireland. Nora has brought in a bundle of clothes given to her by a priest who reports that they have been found on the dead body of a man in the north. The body may be that of the girls' brother Michael. In the meantime, another son Bartley, goes off to the sea-side to search for work. Maurya enters and says she has seen the dead son Michael; the girls explain that this is impossible, for Michael's body has been found in the far north. Then they all hear crying outside and some women enter crossing themselves. They announce that the other son, Bartley, has also just died. Maurya, for the practical custom, begins to think once again about a coffin for her son. His body is brought in on a plank and Maurya greets the event with courage and resignation.

The structure of the play then is virtually non-existent except that there is a pattern of repetition in terms of death. Its absence of formal structure forces us to accept the entire play as just one moment in time. Deaths arrive as they always do but life goes on; at the moment, the old woman seems to possess almost infinite courage and wisdom. There is no slow crescendo toward disaster; the deaths arrive as just a few more out of millions caused by or in the sea every year. We never leave the little kitchen cottage and there are no major actions; instead the structure is designed to be conspicuously informal. This is the rarity of the play and it is our job when analyzing the construction of the play to notice what is rare. The point cannot be too strongly emphasized: every play has its own particular structure no matter how similar that structure may or may not be to the standard patterns. When we read a play like Synge's *Riders to the Sea*, the odds are that structure will not be our greatest concern; instead we will be more interested in the language of the play, which is the language of Irish common folk, and the ways in which the tragedy arises out of the crystallization of a moment in the life of one family. There is as much mood and tone in *Riders to the Sea* as there is in *Antigone*, but the real clues are not to be found in the considerations of structure except to the extent that the lack of formal structure increases the experiences which are recorded in the dialogue. Thus, the student should remember that although every play must be subjected to structural analysis, some plays will not be found to offer us anything particular in their structure; rather, their structures may be so rare that we will notice them briefly, then search for the dimensions of the play which can best be discussed for the purpose of increasing our understanding of the play.

4
Characters

Characters, to begin with, are fictitious creations and the dramatist and also the novelist may both be judged with regard to their ability in the art of characterization. Since a character has no depth before he walks on the stage, the dramatist must invest him with certain distinguishable attributes in a convincing way. We are prepared to accept the reality of these characters for the duration of the play. As we have mentioned in the Introduction, there is no narration or description in a play; instead, all characterization must be presented through dialogue; characters speak about each other and characters speak about themselves—particularly of course about their central emotions, such as love and hate. The combinations of speeches and actions throughout a play, the small asides and jokes, the short angry speeches, the lengthy diatribes, all add up to produce in our minds an understanding of the characters in a drama as people who might really exist. A human being plays the role of a character, thus inviting us to see him as a real person.

Characters in Action. We learn a great deal about the characters in a play by closely observing their actions. How do they behave in different situations? How do they differ from one another in their behaviour when sharing the same situation? How is their action made logical by what we know of their thoughts and motives? How does the action translate into the theme? There are countless questions which can be asked about the characters in action. By answering as many of them as possible we attempt to analyze the characters in terms of their action. We ask, primarily, why a character does what he does and conclude that it must be because he is a certain kind of person. It is part of Othello's character to slap Desdemona in the face when he has become outraged in his jealousy; it is part of Creon's character to shout defiantly at his son; it is part of Faustus' character to mock the Pope. In other words, characters usually do things for certain reasons. We do not always discuss their motivation, because they complete acts which are almost totally unmotivated and are therefore to be explained in some other way; namely, in terms of what is fundamental about them.

Motivation. The fact remains that the larger actions which characters complete in the course of a play have indentifiable motives behind them and thus we as critics have every right and duty to analyze character motivation. Iago decides to bring about the downfall of Othello for a particular reason; he is motivated by a love of power as well as by the desire to be revenged for Othello's promotion of Cassio. Moreover, Iago also "suspects" that Othello has slept with his wife Emilia. Hickey urges others in *The Iceman Cometh* to abandon their pipe-dreams because he is motivated by a fear that all pipe-dreams end in futility or death. Willy Loman is motivated by his own failure in his desire for his sons to be successful. And so forth. Most plays have central motives and in general these are the giant human emotions which motivate most people in real life; a few of the most common are:

- Hope for Reward. A major character desires to bring happiness and prosperity to himself or to those whom he loves; all of his actions are planned to hasten the advent of prosperity and joy. He does virtually nothing except work toward this end.
- Love. Basically, a particular extension of the hope for reward. A character is motivated to certain action because of the love which he has, the love which he wants, or the love which someone has for him. And we must not exclude, again as an extension of the

hope for reward, the motive of self-love ("amour proper").

- Fear of Failure. An inversion of the hope for reward. A character works in a certain fashion because he fears that he will be crushed if he does not. Everything he does is designed to prevent the advent of misery, failure, or literal or spiritual poverty. Sometimes such a motive becomes, in effect, the fear that someone else will fail. Further, sometimes the fear of failure becomes the fear of punishment. A character acts in a certain way because he has been threatened with death or torture if he does not do as he has been told.
- Religious Feelings. Occasionally, but not frequently, we discover a character who is motivated by religious faith. The character acts out of deep feelings and convictions that he is acting as God so directs. His motivation is diminished to the extent that he acts as he thinks he is supposed to act.
- Revenge. Although there are certain plays which we speak of as "revenge tragedies" (The Spanish Tragedy being the usual example, Hamlet another), there are also many other plays in which we find both major and minor characters motivated by the desire to avenge the death of a loved relative or friend. The character usually is willing to lose his own life if necessary, as long as he is able to murder or punish someone who has wronged him.
- Greed. This is a particular kind of motivation in the category of "hope for reward", which becomes an outstanding motive in its own right in many plays; Jonson's Volpone and Shakespeare's The Merchant of Venice afford good examples of dramas in which greed operates as a central motive.
- Jealousy. A final corollary kind of motive, in this case connecting to both love and fear of failure, jealousy operates as one of the most particular and strongest

motives in all drama. Shakespeare's Othello is perhaps the most frequently cited example of a play in which the central character is motivated to action by way of his jealousy. Jealousy—sometimes simply explained as human envy, other times as overwhelmingly bitter hatred—is operative in most human relationships and thus it is not surprising to find it receiving such vast attention in many plays of most of the world's famous dramatists from Molière to Ibsen, from Shaw to Yeats.

The Rounded Character. While we can usually speak of a character's central motive for doing what he does in the course of the play, we can rarely assume that he has one and only one motive. The playwright has the option, of course, to allow his character to have only one motive, but, in general, characters come to us as complex human personalities with many facets. While we may single out Creon's pride as the events of *Antigone* unfold, we must not assume that Creon is only motivated by pride. He has the further motive of wanting to be a good king of Thebes, a position which he has only recently assumed. He wants to have a good relationship with his son. Although pride may lie behind each of his other motives, we cannot leave it unclarified as mere pride. The ramifications of the central motives can usually be detected in lesser ones. Othello's overpowering jealousy connects to his natural, instinctive motivation to excel as a warrior, to maintain his honour, to sustain a tenderness for his new bride, etc. Therefore, we should try to arrive at an understanding of characters as complicated human beings with patterns of motivation rather than single motives. It is of course possible that a dramatist intentionally establishes a character's actions as arising from a single, dominant personality trait. Most frequently we discover such a dominant trait in the sinister desires for evil in traditional villains such as Shakespeare's Iago or Marlowe's Mephistopheles.

Caricature. In literature we speak of a "caricature" when a character's outstanding trait becomes so much exaggerated that it becomes unbelievable. In drama it, generally, comes under the category of "type". In general, we find types more often among minor characters than among major. There is no reason for fully developing a character who has but a small role within a play, just as it would be disastrous and inartistic not to develop quite extensively a major character. This leads to the following consideration.

Active and Passive Characters. Some characters in some plays do not change; they begin as the same kinds of characters as they are in the end. The passive characters are acted upon the events of the play; they are usually static, or unchanging. Conversely, some characters are active. They perform acts, they have large parts in the play, they usually undergo certain changes as a result of the action of the play. Instead of being static they are considered dynamic. Most of the heroes of great tragedies are dynamic characters.

Characters Determining Plot. The essence of a play, its plot, develops out of characters themselves. Things should happen in the play because the characters in the play are the way they are. That is, the plot with all its small episodes and scenes and incidents, its complications and simplifications, is motored by the nature of the characters. Things happen because the characters act in accord with their feelings. We must deal with probability in considering the plot; we must estimate whether characters act as they should in the light of what we know about them. There is a close union then between character and action. Any discussion of plot necessitates discussion of character.

Number of Characters. All the students interested in interpreting/analyzing drama must pay some immediate attention to the number of characters in a play. Obviously, a dramatist cannot include more than he has time enough to develop. In order for a major character to be developed, he must be given certain percentage of the action of the play. Thus, in a play which runs for several hours, only a limited number of its characters can be developed. There is nothing lamentable about minor characters. They are often types because of the necessity of the dramatist's devoting his time to the development of the major characters. The student should make a list of the characters, count them, and group them into major and minor characters, then into men and women. Usually imbalances can be explained. If there are three ladies who may be considered major characters and only one man, the odds may be that the ladies are all competing for the attention of the man, and that the man consequently will be viewed in three separate relationships, one with each of the women, and therefore emerge as a more fully developed character than any one of them. (But it is not always as in the case of Chekhov's *The Three Sisters*, where these three women are not after a man, rather yearning to have change.) In other words, by making a count of the characters and a quick appraisal of the various balances between major and minor, male and female, passive and active, the student automatically places himself in a better position for understanding the play.

The Basic Character Roles. Aside from being lovers, wives, husbands, friends, enemies, etc. characters in dramas have some particular "labels" which are used in analysis/ interpretation. As we have discussed already in the section on Greek tragedy, we often speak of tragic heroes. The tragic hero, as defined by Aristotle, is an eminent man, neither all good nor all bad, who through some flaw in his character brings death or destruction upon himself or upon someone he loves. The main character in the plot of any drama is known as the "protagonist". The tragic hero and the protagonist are the same in a tragedy, for both terms describe the central character. The opponent of the protagonist is known as the "antagonist" or, in the event that the opposing force is not a person, we speak of the antagonistic force. Another important role in drama is that of the friend or confidant (feminine, confidante) of the major character. Often both the hero and the heroine have a confidant and a confidante, respectively, so named because the hero and heroine confide in their friend or serving maid or whoever fills the role. The function of a confidant is to give the hero someone in whom to confide onstage, thus allowing the audience to know his true feelings and motives.

The Characters in Time. When a character walks onto the stage, we know almost nothing about him. One of the dramatist's chief concerns, therefore, becomes the presentation —in one way or another—of some information about the character's past life. We learn through the early speeches of Desdemona and Othello the nature of their courtship. In other words, we must learn action as well as witness action; the same principle of revealing the events prior to the opening of the play operates in revealing deaths offstage. Messengers or sentinels always run onto the stage announcing the death of someone (we saw this to be particularly true in Greek tragedy: remember *Antigone* or *Oedipus the King*). The characters must somehow be brought to be images of real human beings existing in time. They have a past; they are not born in the moment of the play's opening. And, in the same sense, they have a future. When a character dies in a noble, heroic, and at the same time humanly understandable manner, he goes on living in our minds; and if the character lives at the end of the play, we should be able to make some sort of logical speculation regarding his future. Thus, we should always try to determine the extent to which the dramatist has successfully given us the sense of the character in time. And this of course will be accomplished by considering the devices of characterization which the playwright has used.

Devices of Characterization. Every dramatist has at his fingertips a relatively large galaxy of differing devices of characterization. Some of these devices are as follows:

- **The Appearance of the Character.** In the prologue or in the stage directions the playwright often describes the character in the physical sense. We learn from these stage directions what the character looks like and probably how he dresses; when a character walks onto the stage, it is obvious from his appearance whether he is a meticulous or a sloppy person, attractive or unattractive, young or old, small or large, etc. In other words, in the mere appearance of character we locate our first understanding of him.

- **Asides and Soliloquies.** The characters in drama are depicted mainly through dialogue. We learn about the characters as they speak. And specifically, we are apt to understand the characters best when they speak in short asides or in longer soliloquies. On these occasions the character is, in effect, telling the audience of his specific characteristics: if he is a villain, he usually explains his evil intentions or at least his malicious hopes; if he is a lover he offers us poetic statements of devotion; if a hero torn between love and duty, he tells about his conflict, and his resulting anguish or agony. The use of soliloquies and asides is one of the devices/conventions of characterization.
- **Dialogue between Characters.** Not only does the language of the character speaking alone characterize him, but his language when speaking to others also sheds a great deal of light on his personality. If a man speaks one way to his master and another to his underling we can draw various conclusions. If there is a wide disparity between the kind of language used in soliloquies and the kind of language used when talking to others, we are presented usually with a host of implications. Part of our basic understanding of Iago as a dubious, untrustworthy person, for example, derives from the disparity between his candor when speaking alone and his deceitful guile when speaking to Othello or to Cassio.
- **Hidden Narration.** While a character in a play is never directly described by the playwright himself, there are nevertheless descriptions of the characters. One of the devices of the characterization frequently employed is having one character in a play narrate something about another character. The narration is hidden in the sense that it is not the playwright's direct comment; but if Antigone describes her sister we learn about that sister, often just as much as we learn about her through her own speeches

and actions. Of course, sometimes one character's estimation of another is completely wrong; the playwright thus establishes in our mind that a certain character is either foolish or wise before allowing that character to describe other characters. If the character who is describing another is a fool and generally not very perceptive, then we simply alter everything he says about another character in order to arrive at the truth. If a fool thinks someone wise, we generally can assume that that someone is stupid. Thus, there is a great interplay between the playwright's characterization of certain people in the play through their own words and actions, and the characterization through the use of hidden narrations made by one character about another.

- **Language.** It cannot be emphasized too many times that the language of any given character is extremely central to his personality attributes. Not only must we pay close attention to the kind of words which the character uses, but also we must be careful to remember how the character speaks. Is he impassioned? Does he speak in a quiet, timorous way? Does he use flowery language or literal statements of fact? Does he speak rapidly or does he speak in long drawn-out sighs? In short, the way a character speaks and the expressions he uses should always be our first concern. This aspect of characterization is without doubt the most important—and the playwright as well as the critic is well aware of this truth.
- **Character in Action.** As the characters become more involved in the action of the play we quite naturally learn more about them. For once a playwright chooses to have a character act in one way rather than another, we immediately understand that character much better. Motivation usually translates into action in the real world and there is no reason to assume that the same does not hold true in the world

of the characters on the stage. We continually ask ourselves why a certain character behaves in a particular way; as we slowly derive the answers to the why we are able to make conclusions regarding the character's motivation. And our understanding of motivation lies at the heart of analysis/interpretation.

- Sometimes playwrights directly analyze their characters. For example, Ibsen, Osborne and especially Shaw do illustrate their characters in order to avoid certain misconceptions regarding their characters. However, the plays often belie their analysis.

The Development of the Character. Our central task when analyzing character is to delineate and describe the character's development within the play. It is of the utmost importance to understand the way in which the major characters change—or if they do not change, why they do not change—in the course of the play. The best way to analyse the development is to proceed logically and chronologically through the events of the play. What is the character like in the beginning of the play? Why does he act in the way he does at major turning points in the play? What is he like at the end of the play, or if he dies, at the time of his death? Our main concern is to analyse his motivation for acting as he does; then we concentrate on the devices of characterization employed by the dramatist to "educate" us with regards to the nature of the characters.

The Character's Relationship to Other Characters. Part of the character's development is based on the changing nature of his relationship with other characters. If someone who was an enemy slowly becomes a friend, or vice versa, the character naturally needs to adjust to the changing relationship. If we trace the development of a romance, for example, we are literally forced into an evaluation of each of the partners in that romance at different stages of its development. The character's relationship to other characters emerges in both speeches between them, speeches about each other, and, most evidently, in the actions which they share or cause one another to take.

Conclusion. Approaching the play's characters: The student should survey all the characters in the play, making it clear who are the protagonist, antagonist, confidant, fool, wise man, etc. After all of the characters can be seen in their patterns and in their relationships, they can be isolated for individual analysis. By beginning with a consideration of the character in action—i.e. explaining what happens to that character in the course of the play—and then suggesting reasons for that action (motivation), the student can fairly rapidly discover the central truths of the character. By isolating outstanding characteristics of the major characters one is able to develop certain theories of meaning which are implicit in the play. By defining our central task as a delineation of the development of the major characters within the play we will more easily avoid unnecessary discursive wanderings into fruitless speculation regarding the minor characters. As we search for the clues to the various changes in the characters, we should pay attention to the various devices of characterization from which the playwright can choose. Just as we may refer to our list of motives—love, hate, the fear of punishment, the hope for reward, etc.—so we can use as a guide our list of devices of characterization: soliloquies, appearances, and so forth. Perhaps, finally, our minds should come to grips with one dominant question: are the characters in the play, "believable"?

EXAMPLES OF CHARACTERIZATION

Othello. Shakespeare's Othello develops in accordance with the various changes in the development of his jealousy. In the beginning of the play he is seen as a strong and heroic military leader and an able servant of the state of Venice. At the end, immediately prior to his suicide, he has become an animal, mad and jealous and yet humble in his despair after having murdered his innocent wife. Shakespeare characterizes him first by having him appear middle-aged, by presenting him as not only a moor but as a black moor, by having him dress in the costume of a general and in early scenes having to do with the affairs of state. Othello is, however, deceived by appearances. This tragic flaw allows him to be duped by the scheming malicious Iago. Othello becomes increasingly convinced that Desdemona is having an affair with Cassio and eventually murders her. This is what happens in the play: Othello becomes jealous, murders his innocent wife, then commits suicide upon discovery of his mistake. The motivation is simple and uncomplicated, for jealousy is easily defined and understood. Othello's personality, his sense of honour, his pride, all are threatened by one exploding emotion. He develops only as he erupts. He is the active protagonist pitted against Iago, his antagonist. He is superstitious and believes in magic—a trait which makes him all the more vulnerable to Iago's attacks.

Othello is characterized by his language. He speaks in the manner of a professional soldier; he wastes few words and even announces his own inability to speak in fancy words or at great length. His language is bare and factual. In short, Shakespeare has helped to establish a clear picture of Othello the man by carefully having him speak in a certain way. He is further described by the other characters in a thoroughly consistent way. In his dialogues with other characters and in his soliloquies he speaks a uniform language of the typical soldier and man of action. This is our understanding of his past, of what he has always been like, and what he is now like as the curtain rises. His actions within the play are extremely logical in light of what we know about him. He is led into active persecution of someone he believes has wronged his honour.

Willy Loman. Arthur Miller's Willy Loman is sometimes cited as an example of a tragic hero in a bourgeois drama. We recall that the conventional tragic hero in the Aristotelian sense is defined as a noble person who falls from a high to a low estate. Willy Loman is not noble in the conventional way, but he does have a certain representative human dignity. In his suffering is embodied all of the suffering of thousands not very different from him.

In appearance, Willy Loman is easily characterized by the playwright, for he has all the trappings of the onset of old age —or, in different words, is at the end of his middle age. The work he has done has taken its toll not only in a physical sense.

When Willy Loman walks onstage, therefore, part of Miller's characterization is already accomplished.

There is no doubt that Willy Loman is the central character in the play. Willy Loman is a weak man filled with pride and unfulfilled dreams. Biff was to be his salvation but he can never be so. The conclusion is that human weakness and ignorance together only lead to despair and defeat. As radical as suicide may be, it is nevertheless logically understandable as the conclusion to Willy's life. This is perhaps the central horror of the play—that we can easily understand Willy's suicide. The main reason that Willy's death has such a forceful logic is that it is consistent with what we know about him as a character. We see him sinking deeper and deeper in to an unverbalized confession of inadequacy. Willy cannot cope with the world, and he cannot—pathetic as it seems—even understand his own family. Willy is an active character in the sense that he dreams, that he actively encourages Biff to be great.

Willy is of course terribly unrealistic in his approach to life; Miller suggests this aspect of Willy's character by making his dreams more forceful than his present. His contact with reality has been severed by his failures and he can only accept life in the past: the present and future are equally dead to him.

Biff's first real understanding of his father's weakness came with his discovery that his father was ordinary and morally bankrupt. While Willy's external motivation is to be successful in business, his greater motivation is his pride in himself and his family; Biff is to be Willy's last chance to raise the family higher than his neighbour's, the last chance to raise the family into lasting prosperity.

Willy does not develop within the play except in the sense that we gradually understand the subtleties of his character and the mainsprings of his pride and his weakness. His development, such as it is, is largely presented through his lengthy soliloquies. Although surrounded by other members of the family, Willy feels as if he is alone, particularly because he is detached from reality and from the present world. As a part of Willy's character is his sense of living in the past, he is able to utter soliloquies without disrupting the action or location of the play. Miller has suggested that shortly after the play has begun Willy has already reached a depth sometimes only reached by the end of the play in other dramas. Willy begins basically as a failure; he ends as a final and complete failure. His death makes only a marginal or token difference, for he is as good as dead in the very beginning of the play.

Willy is developed in the sense that a painting may slowly be uncovered. All the devices of characterization work toward this style of revelation. Little by little we see why Willy has failed, why he is no longer a good salesman, why he has disappointed Biff, why he wants Happy and Biff to start up a new family business enterprise, why it is so important to him to equalize himself with his neighbour. He is characterized almost entirely through his own speeches and those of the other members of the family, his employer's remarks increase our ability to understand the picture which he himself paints but we never forget that he is the main artist.

Willy is not defined by the action in the play in the sense of present action. He does not do anything at all except allow himself to slide ingloriously into a lost and glorious youth. His action is past and he himself recalls the all-important events which have taken place before the play opens. He falls in a tragic sense because we are purged of our feelings of fear and pity by the time the play comes to a close. We are almost relieved when Willy dies for we know by this time that for him nothing can be worse than continuing in his present existence. We thoroughly understand Willy's fall, his degeneration, and all of his crushing despair, and yet in the light of his infidelity we are not eager to forgive him. We pity him because he has gone about life in a foolish way; all of the premises at the centre of his character are wrong; his certainty that things will get better is an unjustified certainty; his theory that personality alone can make a successful businessman does not translate into the facts of his own business failures. In short, Willy's development and total characterization have at the centre his unrealistic estimation of himself and his world. Just as Othello is so completely saturated with his jealousy, so is Willy saturated with a false pride that is painfully and finally destructively unrealistic.

5

Language and Rhetoric

As we discussed in the Introduction, plays are literary as well as theatrical works of art, and thus it becomes relatively simple for us to study the dramatist's use of language and certain rhetorical devices. When we consider the use of language in plays we are always concerned with the dramatic effectiveness of the playwright's intentions. If a character speaks in a certain way, is he thereby made more dramatic? Is he brought into our central attention? Or does his language establish him swiftly as merely a dramatic "type" with insufficient individuality for becoming dramatic? The language of the play and all of the rhetorical devices which compose style are delivered to the audience necessarily through the medium of the characters' speeches. There is no narration. There is no plain or fancy description; there is first and only dialogue and our analysis of the language of a play is therefore no more than a scrutiny/examination of how certain characters speak.

Language Defining the Characters. As mentioned in the last chapter, the way in which a character is made to speak is a device of characterization. We learn some things about a particular character by observing the way in which she/he speaks. Creon's arguments against his son in *Antigone* are understandably filled with ignorant passion and biting, defiant words. Othello's accusations of Desdemona are filled with the war-like vocabulary of the military plain-speaking commander.

The characters speak in ways not only representative of their individuality but of their kind of people as well. For example, to return to a consideration of Synge's *Riders to the Sea*, all the characters, not just one of them, speak the appropriate language of Irish common folk living on an island. Notice the word order and diction of Maurya's comment—"In the big world the old people do be leaving after them for their sons and children, but in this place it is the young men do be leaving things behind for them that do be old." We see easily and quickly how fundamentally Irish Maurya is simply because of the way she talks. The cadence of "do be leaving after them" gives both individuality and nationality to the speaker in a relatively economical manner. The other characters speak with the same Irish flavour; consider, for example, the opening dialogue of the play:

> *Nora*: (*in a low voice*) Where is she?
>
> Cathleen: She's lying down, God help her, and may be sleeping if she's able.
>
> [NORA *comes in softly, and takes a bundle from under her shawl.*]
>
> *Cathleen: (spinning the wheel rapidly)* What is it you have?
>
> *Nora*: The young priest is after bringing them. It's a shirt and a plain stocking were got off a drowned man in Donegal.
>
> . . . .
>
> *Nora*: We're to find out if it's Michael's they are, sometime herself will be down looking by the sea....

The words and their combinations are essentially Irish and through the language the playwright is able to establish the location of the play, a small island to the west of Ireland; the characters are part of the location and through appropriate language define each other.

Language, Characterization, and Humour. Very early in Shakespeare's famous comedy *A Midsummer Night's Dream*, Shakespeare introduces the company of actors who are to perform the play within the play. They have become one of the most famous and humorous tribes of men in the history of the theatre, and primarily because Shakespeare has delicately used language as a device of characterization. Through Bottom's speeches we quickly see the soul of his personality; there is no substitute for carefully chosen dialogue in establishing humour. Let us consider the introduction of the company of actors, paying particular attention to the speed with which we arrive at an understanding of Bottom.

> *Quince*: Answer as I call you. Nick Bottom, the weaver.
>
> *Bottom*: Ready. Name what part I am for, and proceed.
>
> *Quince*: You, Nick Bottom, are set down for Pyramus.
>
> *Bottom*: What is Pyramus? A lover, or a tyrant?
>
> *Quince*: A lover, that kills himself most gallant for love.
>
> *Bottom*: That will ask some tears in the true performance of it. If I do it, let the audience look to their eyes. I will move storms, I will condole in some measure. To the rest. Yet my chief humour is for a tyrant. I could play Ercles rarely, or a part to tear a cat in, to make all split.
>
> "The raging rocks
> And shivering shocks
> Shall break the locks
> Of prison gates;
> And Phibbus' car
> Shall shine from far,
> And make and mar
> The foolish fates."

This was lofty! Now name the rest of the players. This is Ercles' vein, a tyrant's vein, a lover is more condoling.

> *Quince*: Francis Flute, the bellows-mender.
>
> *Flute*: Here, Peter Quince.
>
> *Quince*: Flute, you must take Thisby on you.
>
> *Flute*: What is Thisby? A wandering knight?
>
> *Quince*: It is the lady that Pyramus must love.

Flute: Nay, faith, let me not play a woman; I have a beard coming.

Quince: That's all one; you shall play it in a mask, and you may speak as small as you will.

Bottom: And I may hide my face, let me play Thisby too. I'll speak in a monstrous little voice, "Thisne! Thisne! Ah Pyramus, my lover dear! Thy Thisby dear, and lady dear!"

Quince: No, no; you must play Pyramus, and Flute, you Thisby.

Bottom: Well, proceed.

Quince: Robin Starveling, the tailor.

Star: Here Peter Quince.

Quince: Robin Starveling, you must play Thisby's mother. Tom Snout, the tinker.

Snout: Here Peter Quince.

Quince: You, Pyramus' father; myself, Thisby's father. Snug, the joiner, you, the lion's part; and I hope, here is a play fitted.

Snug: Have you the lion's part written? Pray you, if it be, give it me, for I am slow of study.

Quince: You may do it extempore, for it is nothing but roaring.

Bottom: Let me play the lion too. I will roar, that I will do any man's heart good to hear me. I will roar, that I will make the Duke say, "Let him roar again; let him roar again."

The script must be presented at this length because, every line increases the characterization so greatly. Bottom's delightful mispronunciation of Thisby as "Thisne" readily underlines his central clumsiness and humorous inept style. His playful ideas couched in plain colloquial language turn him into a familiar friend in only a matter of seconds. Each of the members of the performing company speaks in the briefest of terms, answering "here" when their name is called, making a slight interruption occasionally as when Snug suggests he will need some time to memorize the lion's part—which consists only of a roar. Shakespeare has introduced his band of playful fellows in a direct manner; they become natural because they speak only in an accentuated natural way. Shakespeare's ability to suggest the idea of Bottom is, in effect, his ability not only to give him clever lines but lines phrased in the most appropriate way for the characterization of Bottom as a bumbling self-centred comic actor.

Dialogue Defining Relationships. While dialogue in plays first and foremost defines the characters as they speak, dialogue also is tantamount to the definition of relationships within the play. The language that a particular character uses when talking to one person in the play will be altogether different from the language he uses when talking to another character. For example, the way in which Othello talks to Cassio defines the relationship between them as one existing between a commanding officer and his subordinate officer, while the way in which Othello talks to his new bride defines his marriage relationship as one filled with both love and human tenderness. The dialogue between Othello and Desdemona, in short, defines the relationship between them as husband and wife. As we see the different kinds of language employed by the same character throughout the play, we slowly are led to an understanding of the relationships he has with other characters.

If we recall the sharp dialogue between Creon and Haimon in Sophocles' *Antigone*, we realize that this dialogue serves to define the basic father-son relationship in the play. When Creon reminds Haimon of his judgment of the girl his son had planned to marry, Haimon asserts that his father is wise, then slowly leads into his argument against his father's ignorant action and decision. Haimon slowly begs Creon not to be hardheaded but instead to assert to his superior wisdom by reversing his original decision. To Creon's defense that his judgment has behind it the rights of kings, Haimon introduces the rights sponsored by divine judging. In short, the father and son work slowly through a logically connected series of arguments. As they speak, it becomes increasingly obvious that

Creon and Haimon argue just like all fathers and sons do argue; the normality of their father-son relationship is thus clearly established through the dialogue as the conversation moves from the polite to the angry and from discussion to argument. In all plays, relationships are—or at least let us say should be—clearly delineated through the nature of the shifts in the dialogue. The various modulations color the subtleties of the relationship—as, for example, when it needs to be shown that a character has ambivalent feelings toward another character and thus the turns of the dialogue revolve around both love and hate; when words of love are offered, there is a corollary suggestion if not affirmation, of a supplementary and a converse emotion. The student should be able to take any extended dialogue between two or more characters and show the ways in which the language used in the dialogue define the relationships of the play.

Figurative Language. All playwrights—in fact all writers—make use of figurative language, i.e. playwrights state the things in other than literal ways. The playwright explains his ideas by the use of analogies which can be presented in different ways. An analogy points up the similarity between one thing and another, thus drawing increased attention to something. If we say that one thing is like another, we are employing a simile to present our analogy; for example, if we write "the sun is like a hot dime in the sky" we have figuratively depicted the sun by the use of a simile (similes are introduced by "like" or "as"). The other basic kind of analogous expression is a metaphor; when we use a metaphor we say that one thing is something else, at least in a figurative (analogous) way. Thus, if we rephrased our earlier example to read "the sun is a hot dime in the sky", we have presented the same idea by way of a metaphor. Similes and metaphors are at the heart of figurative expression and most dramatists employ them freely and profusely in the speeches of most of their characters. Similes and metaphors are used to make language both more colourful and more dramatic. There are colourless kinds of figures of speech aside from the two basic ones. When examining the speeches of various characters the student should pay particular attention to any use of some of the following:

(a) **Allegory:** Or the use of extended metaphor; everything being said on the literal level has an obvious meaning on another level.

(b) **Alliteration:** Or the repetition of similar sounds in words placed closely together. Often, for dramatic effect, a character will deliver a long line in which every sound starts with the same letter or sound.

(c) **Antithesis:** Or oxymoron or the use of opposite terms very closely together. In order to create (or heighten) either humour or tension a playwright will present ironic couplings of opposites—"hateful love", "bitter sweetness", "sad splendour", etc. Antithesis is very common in Elizabethan and Restoration plays.

(d) **Cacophony:** Or the presentation of harshly blending sounds; cacophony is really another word for *dissonance*; sometimes a character speaks a language filled with cacophony in order to establish himself as either a 'rough' character or as one who does not know how to speak sweetly.

(e) **Epithet:** Or a word or a phrase used to characterize someone in the briefest possible way. We judge epithets by considering how appropriate it is for describing the particular character in the light of what we know about him from what the other characters say.

(f) **Euphemism:** Or an elaborate way of saying something. Sometimes characters use embellished language, making everything seem more decent/ respectable/harmless/refined/genteel than in reality or than when described in literal language. A euphemism is a common (or ordinary) figure of speech. In other words, euphemism is a method of excluding harsh/unpleasant facts. Example, she is in the "family way" or "this is the powder room".

(g) **Euphony:** It is the use of sweetly agreeing sounds in speech (the opposite of cacophony), or the harmonious sounds which are pleasing.

(h) **Paradox:** Or the use of self-contradictory ideas, words, or images. Paradox is used to emphasize or draw attention to some particular aspect of an object or person.

(i) **Periphrasis or Circumlocution:** The longwinded roundabout saying something. Often a character will deliberately 'stretch out' his remarks for dramatic effect. Often we discover a character using periphrasis as a means of building up slowly to his main point; we may become so bored with this tedious manner of expression that when a concrete idea finally comes, it often explodes into our attention.

(j) **Personification:** Or the attribution of life-like or human attributes to inanimate objects or ideas. When love "flies", an abstraction is involved in physical completion (thus a figurative rather than literal expression). Dramatists often address the moon as a lady or a kingdom as a friend, etc. in each instance bestowing life on the inhuman.

(k) **Imagery (Images):** These are imaginative ways of describing people and objects. Instead of simply presenting the literal description, the playwright associates the thing described with other things as have been noted in our discussion of certain plays, imagery is apt to be central to our understanding of the meaning of a play. Let us recall certain aspects: simile, in which we have a literally presented analogy between two things (introduced by "like" or "as"); metaphor, in which we have an 'implied' analogy between two things; images, which are usually appealing to our senses; and symbols, which are intellectual as well as sensuous. Most images, as with similes, metaphors, and symbols, are designed to draw our attention to certain characteristics of one thing through an association of that thing with other things. Often we will find in drama the alternation of light and darkness; images support certain moral values, as light tends to become associated with goodness and darkness associated with evil (there is a name for the imagery of light and darkness, incidentally: *chiaroscuro*). Images are designed to reinforce characterization and meaning, and as certain kinds of images are repeated we can often talk about patterns of imagery, or recurrent images. We can notice the disease imagery of *Hamlet*, the imagery of magic in *Othello*, the animal imagery in *King Lear*. In general imagery is more commonly discovered in tragedy than in comedy; comedy often relies more heavily on social statement than on imagery for supporting meaning.

These then are a few of the more common figures of speech: simile, metaphor, allegory, alliteration, antithesis, cacophony, epithet, euphemism, euphony, imagery, paradox, periphrasis and personification. The important problem for the student to solve is the determination of the extent to which a playwright uses or relies upon figurative rather than literal language. In many plays characters simply speak in plain, straightforward terms, while in others they speak in longwinded baroque or ornate terms. Most plays lean on one way or the other and within most plays there are usually some characters who use figurative language a great deal while there are others who hardly use it at all. The language of a play is after all no more than the language of the characters—and they are often characterized merely by the extent to which they make use of figurative language. Let us briefly examine a few speeches built around figures of speech.

EXAMPLES OF FIGURATIVE LANGUAGE

Shakespeare's *Richard III.* The soliloquies delivered by major characters throughout Shakespeare's plays afford countless examples of figurative speech; one such example is discovered in the opening soliloquy by Richard in *Richard III*

Now is the winter of our discontent

Made glorious summer by this sun of York,
And all the clouds that lowered upon our house
In the deep bosom of the ocean buried.

. . . .

Grim-visages war hath smoothed his wrinkled front,
And now, instead of mounting barbed steeds
To fright the souls of fearful adversaries,
He capers nimbly in a lady's chamber
To the lascivious pleasing of a lute.
But I, that am not shaped for sportive tricks,
Nor made to court an amorous looking glass;
I, that am rudely stamped, and want love's majesty
To strut before a wanton ambling nymph

. . . .

I am determined to prove a villain
And hate idle pleasures of these days. (ll. 1-31)

The opening two lines contain a triple pun: Edward IV was the son of the Duke of York; he bore a sun as his representative shield; and he was also the bright rising sun of the party in power, the Yorkists. Discontent is represented figuratively (here metaphorically) by winter, while supposed happiness is represented figuratively by the opposite, the sun. The pun on "son" makes the figure even more appropriate. In addition to this use of metaphor and symbolism, we find the personification of war. An abstract term, "war", becomes "grim-visaged" and no longer rides into battle but instead courts lust; thus "war" is ironically used as a term for Edward IV. Then as move into Richard's remarks on his deformity and ugliness, we find him using figurative language in other ways; he speaks of his inability to court a mirror—which is euphemistic way of saying that he is too ugly to look at himself in a mirror, or that mirrors themselves would not permit it. He speaks, further, of himself as "rudely stamped", as if he were a poorly minted coin. People are of course not stamped, but image makes his ugliness more familiar to us. Richard is mis-stamped, an accident, an unfortunate freak of nature, and his language aptly characterizes him because there is a reliance on dramatic images and figures.

Shakespeare's *Coriolanus*. Characters establish their own identities through the use of figurative language, but just as frequently do they describe each other in figurative terms in order to enlarge our picture of the chief characters. Such is the case, for example, when Cominius describes the valour of Coriolanus in battle in Shakespeare's famous *Coriolanus*:

His pupil age
Man-entered thus, he waxed like a sea,
And in the brunt of seventeen battles since,
He lurched all swords of the garland. For this last,
Before and in Corioli, let me say,
I cannot speak in home. He stopped the flyers,
And by his rare example made the coward
Turn terror into sport. As weeks before
A vessel under sail, so men obeyed,
And fell below his stem. His sword, death's stamp,
Where it did mark, it took. From face to foot
He was a thing of blood, whose every motion
Was timed with dying cries. Alone he entered
The mortal gate of the city, which he painted
With shunless destiny; aidless came off,
And with a sudden reinforcement struck
Corioli like a planet. Now all's his. (II, ii, ll. 102-18)

The use of figurative language is wonderful throughout the description. We first find a euphemistic way of saying that Coriolanus became a man; then we come to a simile (introduced by 'like') drawing an analogy between Coriolanus' rising valour and the swelling of the sea; then a homely expression (meaning roughly, I can't do him justice). Then we arrive at a second, larger simile (introduced by "as") in which the men under Coriolanus fall into subservience just as seaweed falls under the onrushing ship. The second simile is prepared for us by a hyperbole—another common dramatic figure of speech—in which the brave men turn terror into sport because they are so greatly inspired by their leader Coriolanus. It is particularly interesting to notice the way picture of

Coriolanus' courage rising like the sea turns into the picture of Coriolanus himself sailing powerfully like a ship upon that very sea. As the speech of description continues we have the image of Coriolanus as a large bloody engine trampling down its enemies. The entire description of Coriolanus as a warrior and dreaded enemy to those he attacks is made brilliant and exciting through the use of various figures; the blend of hyperbole, simile, personification, etc. produces a large extended exaggeration of Coriolanus' might that would not easily be made convincing through ordinary literal description.

Sheridan's Mrs. Malaprop in *The Rivals*. Sometimes figurative language takes on very special duties in the line of characterization. Often we discover the widespread use of double entendre or even puns, as in the opening two lines in *Richard III*. The special effects of language are, to a certain extent, dealt with in the next chapter. But the student should at least realize that figurative language sometimes is misdirected or used incongruously entirely for comic effects. Such is the case with Mrs. Malaprop, the now famous ill-speaking lady in Sheridan's play *The Rivals*. Malapropism refers to an incorrectly used word: although pronounced in a satisfactory, and even expert manner, the meaning of the word is not understood. This is the case when Mrs. Malaprop asks Lydia to "illiterate" someone from her memory (she is of course thinking "obliterate"), when she refers to an "allegory" on the banks of the Nile (thinking of an alligator). A figure of speech, in other words, can sometimes be misused for special effects. We will see the implications of such usage even more clearly when we consider irony later on.

Having examined several passages relying strongly on figurative language, we should be able to understand its centrality, i.e. in most plays we will find such languages used consistently throughout for purposes of speedy characterization, since a dramatist is limited in time. If some of the figures are repeated at certain intervals throughout the play, we in the audience are able to form a 'lasting impression' of that character. How quickly we understand the jealousy of Othello, the valour of Coriolanus, or the comic manner of

Bottom—and largely because Shakespeare is the master of writing dialogue based on figurative expressions.

HIGH AND LOW LANGUAGE

In most plays we are able to determine whether the language on the whole is "high" or "low". By "high" we mean lofty, formal, rhetorically polished language and even language which relies strongly on fanciful expressions and by "low" we mean simple, plain, and unadorned language. It is important to identify the range of the language in order to determine the conventions within which the playwright is working. Because one of our first tasks—as previously pointed—is to define the world of the play, it is essential that we have some immediate grasp of the general kind of language used throughout the play. Obviously not all of the characters within a play speak the same kind of language. For example, there are three kinds of language used by different sets of characters within Shakespeare's *A Midsummer Night's Dream*—that of the Duke and Hippolyta, that of Oberon and the fairies, and that of the actors company of Bottom, Snug, Quince, and others. Nevertheless the play as a whole can be considered as written in the language of romantic comedy; while Theseus speaks in what we would call "high" language and Bottom in what we would obviously call "low" language, we understand that the basic idiom of the play is closer to low than high. Conversely, although there are crude or comic remarks throughout *Othello*, the language is generally closer to "high" than "low".

Addison's *Cato*. Addison's famous pseudo-classical tragedy, *Cato*, written in 1713, affords a good example of a play which is almost wholly written in high language; the rhetoric is full-blown or lofty; the words are frequently long; there is little colloquialism or short expression; in all the play is written in a high style (we can interchange the terms "style" and "language" when speaking of "high" and "low" because it is the use of the language that determines the style of the play). Consider for example a dialogue between Lucia and Portius in Act III. We recall that Lucia is torn in half because she loves both of Cato's sons—Portius and Marcus. In the following conversation Lucia is explaining that if she and Portius were to follow natural inclinations of their love they would bring great unhappiness and disaster to the rest of the family; notice how the style is high throughout, how both Lucia and Portius grope to make their expression equal to their feelings:

> *Lucia*: Did not I see your brother Marcus here?
> Why did he fly the place, and shun my presence?
> *Portius*: Oh, Lucia, language is too faint to show
> His rage of love; it preys upon his life;
> He pines, he sickens, he despairs, he dies:
> His passions and his virtue lie confused,
> And mixed together in so wild a tumult,
> That the whole man is quite disfigur'd in him.
> Heav'ns! Would one think 'twere possible for love
> To make such a ravage in a noble soul!
> Oh Lucia, I'm distrest! My heart bleeds for him;
> Ev'n now, while thus I stand blest in thy presence,
> A secret damp of grief comes o'er my thoughts,
> And I'm unhappy, though thou smil'st upon me.
> *Lucia*: How will thy guard thy honour in the shock
> Of love and friendship! Think betimes, my Portius,
> Think how the nuptial tie, that might ensure
> Our mutual bliss, would raise to such a height
> Thy brother's griefs, as might perhaps destroy him.

Lucia's first phrases, "fly the place" and "shun my presence", establish her rhetoric as expansive—and this expansiveness is developed throughout the speech by Portius; for example, notice the gradual enlargement carried out by the line "he pines, he sickens, he despairs, he dies". The words, descriptive and to the point, have an additive effect so that by the time we arrive at "dies" we almost accept the term literally. To be bothered by love becomes having your soul ravaged by love; to explain that he is becoming upset, Portius says in full-blown splendour, "A secret damp of grief comes o'er my thoughts." The point is clear without further elaboration; throughout the dialogues of *Cato* the language is written in a high style—and this is perfectly appropriate for the writing of classical tragedy. We recall, for example, some of the speeches of Sophocles' *Antigone*.

Using Allusions. Another aspect of high style is the use of allusions. The mere mention of faraway exotic-sounding places transports the audience quickly into a higher realm; the allusion to places and people presents a sense of grandeur and elevates the import of a speech. As an example, consider briefly the first speech in the play delivered by Cato; he arrives in the very opening of the second act to address the senate on the subject of Caesar's approach toward Utica:

> Fathers, we once again are met in council.
> Caesar's approach has summon'd us together,
> And Rome attends her fate from our resolves;
> How shall we treat this blood, aspiring man?
> Success still follows him and backs his crimes:
> Pharsalia gave him Rome; Egypt has since
> Received his yoke, and the whole Nile is Caesar's.
> Why should I mention Juba's overthrow,
> And Scipio's death? Numidia's burning sands
> Still smoke with blood. 'Tis time we should decree
> What course to take. Our foe advances on us,
> And envies us ev'n Libya's sultry deserts.
> Fathers, pronounce your thoughts: are they still fixt
> To hold it out and fight it to the last?

As Cato speaks of the places where Caesar has already left his mark, we are on the one hand more aware of the great threat which he poses to Cato and to Utica, and on the other hand we are almost mysteriously swept up into a higher realm through the language itself; there is a certain formality and seriousness in the allusions which give Cato's speech an immediacy, an urgency. In our introduction to this chapter we highlighted the fact that we are always concerned with the dramatic effectiveness of the playwright's intentions: the allusions of Cato's speech are intended to transport us immediately into a larger world of action and decision where honour rules and the stakes are high; Cato's opening speech becomes dramatically effective larger through the high style of the language; he is speaking in a certain way in order that Addison may make him more dramatic as the central title character. Because our analysis of a play is an analysis of how characters speak—at least when we are directing our attention to the language of the play—we must always try to gauge the dramatic effectiveness of the style, whether it be high or low.

COLLOQUIAL LANGUAGE

One very specialized use of figurative language is that discovered in everyday common speech; the colloquial language is of course written in a "low" style, as we can well recall from O'Neill's *The Iceman Cometh*. The men in the bar, Rocky, the prostitutes—all speak in ordinary ways, relying quite extensively on their normal figures of expression. Colloquial writing is that which uses this language of ordinary speech; the language is thus rude or unadorned.

Shakespeare's *Henry IV, Part I*: Most of the dialogue between Falstaff and others in Shakespeare's historical play *Henry IV, Par I* is written in colloquial language. When a character remarks, for example, "the devil rides upon a fiddlestick", he is using the kind of homespun expression which he uses all the time. There is no attempt to create poetry out of such expressions; rather the playwright attempts to demonstrate the essential poetry existent in our colloquial kinds of language. Most of our creative expressions have become almost literal substitutes over time; "a stone's throw" is not a confusing figure of speech but instead practically an absolute equivalent of "nearby". If we examine almost any of the colloquial speeches from *Henry IV, Part I* it will be clear that such ordinary language has a great deal of originality of expression; and the more the dramatist can capture the flavour of that creative language, the better playwright he is. Let us examine briefly a speech from the second act in which Prince Hal playfully criticizes the obese Falstaff:

> There is a devil haunts thee in the likeness of
>
> An old fat man, a tun of man is thy companion. Why dost thou converse with that trunk of humours, that bolting hutch of beastliness,
>
> that swollen parcel of dropsies, that huge bombard
>
> of sac, that stuffed cloak-bag of guts, that roasted

manningtree ox with the pudding in his belly, that
reverend vice, that grey iniquity, that father ruffian,
that vanity in years? Wherein is he good
but to taste sack and drink it? wherein neat and
cleanly but to carve capon and eat it? wherein
cunning but in craft? wherein crafty but in
villainy? Wherein villainous but in all things?
Wherein worthy but in nothing? (II, iv, ll. 492-505)

In these fourteen lines we discover all the energy and even logical progression used in common "low" speech. Falstaff's central sensuality, his carnal pleasures and his egotism and his humorous worthlessness to society are all underlined in a minimum of terms; words like "guts" and "swollen" acquire even more than their usual expressiveness because they are so numerous. The passage is crowded with words of a common nature; the poetry, if we want to call it that, exists in the realism of the description. Colloquial language, as opposed to high and noble language, captures the essence of a different type of character. And this leads us to a final consideration, the conventions of dramatic language.

CONVENTIONS OF DRAMATIC LANGUAGE

It is a given assumption that certain kinds of characters speak in certain ways, i.e. there are many conventions of dramatic language. Fools always speak in riddles, kings of war and honour, etc. One of the considerations when approaching the language of any play is whether or not the language of a particular character is appropriate to his type. Does the ruffian speak in flowery language or the fair princess in the coarse language of a prostitute? As a rule, playwrights tend to conform to the conventions of dramatic language and thus some of their preliminary work is done for them. In an Elizabethan tragedy there are inevitable soliloquies by one or more of the noble, heroic characters. There are always protestations and vows of vengeance in revenge plays; there are always asides in comedies of manners; there are always sharp retorts in domestic tragedies. And so forth. Each kind of play is itself a convention—as we mentioned when surveying the characteristics of Dryden's "heroic" plays. And within each kind of play there are always certain character relationship, from master and servant to man and wife. Certain kinds of characters in certain kinds of plays must speak in certain kinds of language. If this axiom is kept firmly in mind the student will be able to begin his analysis of a play's language by inquiring first into the kind of play. There is nothing meager or overly simplistic about pointing out that a character speaks in a way conventional to his type; if he is a professional soldier we would be surprised to discover him talking like anything other than a professional soldier. If a knight speaks like a man in the street we are outraged and perhaps even offended. We in the audience have as much respect for conventions as the playwright himself.

Conventions and Audience Expectations. The expectations of the audience must be fulfilled to some extent. This does not mean simply that we want property restored to a rightful heir in the end of a play which has promised and logically foreshadowed such an ending. Expectations apply to language as well. Audience expectations are, in effect, one of the dramatist's tools. Because the playwright knows that the audience expects princesses and heroes to speak in certain ways, he writes their speeches accordingly. Because comic relief and a relief from serious language is often needed and expected, the dramatist writes scenes with fools, servants, maids, and other "lower" characters with humorous, often colloquial, dialogues.

There is nothing more central to a play's characters than the ways in which they speak. Language itself is a plurality or modes of expression and the playwright really has no excuse not to have characters of different kinds easily talking in different ways. This is the general rule. It follows that if all of the characters in a play have approximately the same social background and intellectual credentials in general, they will probably talk in similar ways. The members of Willy Loman's family speak a common language; it is conventional for most people of the same family to share certain linguistic habits. At the same time the parents speak slightly differently than the boys. But in any case, for the most part their language is a shared experience and the audience would be inappropriately surprised to find too wide a divergence, a divergence which could not be logically understood by differences in age, education, sex, etc. In Shakespeare's *A Midsummer Night's Dream* we have noted how there are central differences in the kinds of language spoken by the different kinds of characters. The audience expects Theseus to speak in lofty sonorous language, in regal pomp, and high style adjectives. At the same time, the audience would be understandably surprised if Bottom or Snug spoke the same language as Theseus. Shakespeare is in fact making fun of the conventions of dramatic language in the play within the play; Thisby and Pyramus speak as highly romanticized young lovers, similar to Romeo and Juliet. Thus, Flute says, "Most radiant Pyramus, most lily-white of hue,/ Of colour like the red rose on triumphant brier", etc. Shakespeare is fully aware of the humorous implications of conventional ways in which the audience expects certain kinds of characters to speak. Bottom and his company of actors are in their language within the strictest boundaries of a convention—and so are Titania, and Puck, and Thisby and Pyramus. Each kind of character is speaking in the way in which the audience expects him to speak. Conventions translate into audience familiarity at every turn; we in the audience expect linguistic conventions and are disappointed if characters speak in the "wrong" way. Usually we refer to either action or language when we say that someone is "out of character"; by the converse logic, we want characters to be "in character", i.e. within the conventions which dictate the boundaries within which they can express themselves.

A Play is to be Seen. We have been examining some of the important considerations bearing on the language of the play—which in general we study through the medium of the printed word. But in conclusion we should always remember that a play is to be seen, that we must imagine, as readers, precisely how certain speeches are delivered on the stage. What is the tone? What is the level (loudness)? In the prologue to his 1722 play, *The Conscious Lovers* (one of the most important examples of the sentimental comedies of the early eighteenth century), Richard Steele reminded the audience: "It must be remembered a play is to be seen, and is made to be represented with the advantage of action, nor can appear but with half the spirit without it; for the greatest effect of a play in reading is to excite the reader to go see it; and when he does so, it is then a play has the effect of example and precept." In other words, whenever we are directing our attention to the language of the play—which we always must—we should try to keep reminding ourselves that the language is being spoken in the dramatist's mind and thus should be in ours as well.

6

Further Dimensions and Devices

Dramatic Irony. Often in a play we have a situation in which the character does not fully understand the significance of his actions or statements. The characters' actions have a relevance to him which he does not perceive, and when this happens we describe the situation as one of dramatic irony. How often we observe a character "unknowingly" laying out plans which will harm him; how often we in the audience recognize the humour of something which the character does not even know is funny. Dramatic irony results through the imbalance of knowledge between the character and the audience; the irony rests in the incompletion of the meaning of words and actions as they are considered by the character. Only we in the audience see "the full picture"; our understanding is often enhanced because we, but not a particular character, were "present" in a previous scene. In fact, because we watch (or read) all of the scenes in the play, while every character is sometimes absent, we know more than any one of them and as much as all of them. Dramatic irony is used very widely by playwrights of all ages, primarily because it is a device by means of which the audience and the playwright can be brought into a shared secret; we acquire an immediate knowledge of the characters and revel in knowing things which they do not.

Mistaken Identity. One specialized irony is that of mistaken identity. Some plays in fact have plots entirely dependent on the device of mistaken identity. In this situation, some of the characters on the stage are simply unaware of the identity of the other characters while the audience knows who everybody is. Shakespeare's *Twelfth Night* makes use of this device through the character of Viola. An even better example is provided by the well-known eighteenth century comedy, Oliver Goldsmith's *She Stoops to Conquer.*

Mistaken Identity and the Plot of *She Stoops to Conquer.* Tony Lumpkin sends Marlow and Hastings to the home of Mr. Hardcastle telling them that it is an inn. Marlow's father Sir Charles Marlow and Hardcastle are very old friends and Hardcastle has been expecting young Marlow as a houseguest. When Marlow treats Hardcastle as a common inn-keeper, we in the audience are able to laugh continuously; but Marlow does not realize the mistaken identity of Hardcastle; who has no way of knowing that he is being taken for an inn-keeper and thus naturally finds Marlow's orders very uncivil; Marlow has no way of knowing that the inn-keeper is really Hardcastle and thus finds him tiring in his attempts to be friendly. The comedy of the mistaken identity is rich; the "device" is well-chosen and apt.

To amplify this mistaken identity Goldsmith introduces another. He has Marlow flirt with Kate Hardcastle as if she were a common inn-keeper's servant girl; he has no way of knowing that she is really Miss Hardcastle. Thus, later he denies having ever made protestations of love and affection toward Kate and we in the audience—and Kate herself—know very well that Marlow has unknowingly made such amorous protestations toward her. Again, the same way in which one character mistakes the identity of another provides the central humour of the play. The idea of the play is that Kate, as the proper young lady, is unable to find a husband in Marlow because he is intimidated by her social presence; therefore she becomes a common flirtatious wench whom Marlow finds irresistible; she has "stooped to conquer" and the play has been made successful all through the careful use of the device of mistaken identity.

Pathos. Pathos in drama, and in ordinary literary forms as well, is the quality which moves the audience to pity, tenderness, sympathy, or sorrow. Usually we observe pathos in situations where there is a helpless character, one who suffers because of undeserved sadness. When the character is caught up in sorrow and we pity her (more often "her" than "him") we consider her pathetic. There is a whole genre of "pathetic tragedy" in which the hero or heroine is, in effect, made too pathetic; our pity becomes excessive and consequently less sincere; such is the case in the eighteenth century pathetic tragedy *The Tragedy of Jane Shore* by Nicholas Rowe. We recall from our discussion of the principles of classical tragedy as outlined by Aristotle in his *Poetics* that a true tragedy should move us to pity and fear; thus the element of pathos is present in most tragedies, although to varying degrees. Occasionally, a playwright fails in his attempts to achieve pathos—either intentionally or unintentionally—and sometimes the character becomes "bathetic", or in a situation of "bathos". Usually, bathos occurs because the author falls short of his intentions, either by treating a commonplace idea or image with excessive elaboration, or by trying too hard to make us feel pity—the result being that we cannot keep from laughing.

Sentimentalism. When a playwright tries to produce or reflect an overbalance of emotion, he is usually creating a situation of "sentimentalism". In addition to excessive emotionalism, sentimentalism also means excessive goodness. The honest, weepy-eyed, faithful, chaste, virtuous daughter is often a sentimental character because she is filled with uncontrolled emotions of tenderness, honesty, etc. while at the same time infinitely attracted to moral good. In the so-called "sentimental comedies" of the eighteenth century, the heroes and heroines expressed themselves too subjectively, while at the same time they exhibited only the most honourable and virtuous intentions. The hero is always moral and without bad habits; at the same time, he feels everything very "deeply". The problem with sentimentalism is that the audience often concludes by being embarrassed by both the excess and the righteousness of the emotions displayed on the stage.

Parody. Quite often a playwright writes a play which is an obvious burlesque of another play, usually of a serious nature; this burlesque is known as a parody. Usually the action, kinds of characters, and language are all satirized in a parody—an excellent example being Henry Fielding's famous parody of the heroic tragedies of Dryden in his *The Tragedy of Tragedies*, or *The Life and Death of Tom Thumb the Great*. In this parody Fielding humorously satirizes some forty-two plays by mocking or burlesquing their seriously employed dramatic conventions of character and speech.

Reversal. Reversal is the term we use to describe the dramatic turning point in the fortune of the play's hero; reversal is the exact point in the plot when suddenly the hero is directed toward a different fate, toward a fate which up until this exact point in the play he had no idea was in store for him; often the opposite of what is expected also known as *peripetia*.

Recognition. This is the way in which we describe a plot where the hero experiences his reversal or *peripetia* largely because of some new "recognition". Some new knowledge is added to the play, either by the playwright or else discovered suddenly by a character (while we have known it all along); this new knowledge has been kept a secret either completely by the author or from one character by another (but therefore not from the audience). Recognition plots are used in both comedy and tragedy; we can recall our discussion of mixed identity in Goldsmith's *She Stoops to Conquer* or of Creon's reversal in *Antigone*. It should further be noted that we refer to the scene in which this central recognition occurs as a "recognition scene". Many plays have some central recognition scene leading to reversal or *peripetia*, but some plays have several such scenes, introducing several parcels of new information gradually rather than all at once; this is often the case, for example, in any kind of mystery play (or story).

Denouement. The final revelation of a play is usually referred to as the denouement; this is both a necessity and device in almost all plays. If a mystery, we are offered the solution; if a case of mistaken identity, we are given true identities. The denouement is an effective dramatic device because it allows the playwright to build up toward it in a suspenseful way. In the conclusion of a play the audience's mounting curiosity must be finally and fully satisfied. Denouement appears in both comedies as well as tragedies, though as discussed in an earlier chapter, in tragedy it is often the catastrophe. In any case, denouement should always be referred to when discussing a play, no matter what the final events may be—the reuniting of separated lovers, the revelation of a disguised character, etc.

Didacticism. When a playwright is consciously "lecturing" to us on certain moral principles—and generally the superiority of moral good—he is usually "didactic". Some playwrights have some lesson to teach us and through both the actions and the speeches of the characters the playwright presents his argument. We observe a play as students; we go to college while in the theatre to the extent that the playwright makes it obvious that he wants it to adopt a certain kind of social behaviour or endorse certain of his attitudes toward man and toward society. If the didacticism of the playwright is associated very strongly with a certain well-known system or doctrine (political, philosophical, religious), the playwright and the play are often described as "doctrinaire".

Domestic Tragedy. While we have examined at some length the principles of classical tragedy, we have not noted the appearance of certain tragedies which are based on the lives of common, ordinary people and are generally called "Domestic tragedies" (or even bourgeois drama). There are certain plays throughout the history of the English theatre which are addressed themselves to the kinds of tragedy common in the lives of everyday contemporary people. Thomas Heywood's *A Woman Killed with Kindness* is a good example of an Elizabethan Domestic tragedy. This play, like others of Heywood, was apparently very popular with the bourgeois. John Frankford discovers his wife Anne in bed with his trusted friend Wendoll when he returns from a business trip.

Frankford accuses his wife of infidelity, even before their children, and decides to kill her with kindness by simply making her live in his manor with servants but unable to see him. The play is filled with all the marital strife of a television soap-opera and yet at the same time assumes the dimensions of tragedy. In the course of the play infidelity leads to death, loss of honour is prevented through the honour of someone else (in the sub-plot); the play runs the gamut of marital temptations and infidelity; the good husband is wronged as is so common in domestic tragedies. In the eighteenth century, domestic tragedy reappeared, largely as a contemporary reaction against the heroic plays of Dryden, Otway and Lee and was filled not only with problems of everyday marriages but with vast sentimentalism. In more recent times there have been some domestic tragedies such as one we have looked at very closely, Arthur Miller's *Death of a Salesman.* Willy Loman is not highborn and yet his suffering runs as deep, leading to a ruin no less pitiful and tragic than that of Lear.

Blank Verse. Because so many plays have been written in blank verse, the student will do well to remember exactly what it is: the lines in the most of the speeches are unrhymed and contain ten syllables alternating unstressed and stressed ones (iambic pentameter); consider these lines by Lucius from a play we have already mentioned, Addison's *Cato*:

> My thoughts, I must confess, are turn'd on peace.
> Already have our quarrels fill'd the world
> With widows and with orphans: Scythia mourns
> Our guilty wars, and earth's remotest regions
> Lie half unpeopled by the feuds of Rome:
> 'Tis time to sheathe the sword, and spare mankind.

It should be noted that in blank verse, or unrhymed iambic pentameter, some lines conform more rigidly to the meter than others—consider the strong cadence of the final line, and then compare that to the third, where "Scythia" creates some problems of stress. Furthermore, within a play which is written primarily in blank verse there are many speeches written in ordinary language, particularly short ones of interrupting dialogue (announcements, messengers, sudden deaths, etc.).

Blank verse has more or less been finally approved by succeeding generations as the very best form of verse in drama. Within the speeches there are certain other things to be noted—the location in the line of the caesura (pause, breathing place), the use of the run-on-line, and the changes in the diction. The acknowledged masters of dramatic blank verse are Shakespeare and Marlowe.

Irony, mistaken identity, reversal, the list of further dimensions of drama seems endless. But gradually the student will find almost all of the expressions passing into his common vocabulary when writing about certain plays; no one of the terms is indispensable. Analysis or interpretation can be made without any of them, but knowing the right critical terms can be of great help, not only in articulating your own ideas but in helping you to discover ideas themselves by asking, for example, "What is the irony in this play?"

7

Interpreting the Play

When we interpret or analyze a play we are not merely concerned with the functioning of its various necessary components such as action, characters, structure, and patterns of imagery. Our ultimate task is always the explanation of what the play "means". What significance is attached to the action, the characters, or the imagery? Quite fortunately there is usually a central theme which can be discovered. However, the implications, the subtleties, and the nuances of explaining this theme all make up part of our interpretation of the play. One of the truly exciting aspects of literary criticism is the diversity of interpretations which can be inferred from a work of art. *Hamlet* comes to mind as one of the most talked-about literary works and characteristically, the pages of criticism far exceed the pages of the play. When the student is first learning to analyze a play from the point of view of interpreting its meaning, it helps to keep in mind certain basic relationships which playwrights are apt to explore. Some of the most frequent ones follow.

Man and Nature. Many playwrights explore the relationship between man and natural world in one way or another; obviously some plays do not really touch on this relationship at all. The student should ask of a play, is there any statement being made about man and nature? Often he will be able to conclude that the playwright considers nature a hostile or destructive force. Man is seen unable to cope with an oppressive environment. In Synge's short Irish drama which we examined earlier, *Riders to the Sea*, there is a strong accusation of the sea. Many people of the same family, as well as many friends in other families, have all been killed by drowning: Synge implies that by living on an island off the coast man places himself in a position where he can be ruined by the sea. The statement is really something along the lines of—how small a thing is man, how finite, especially when compared to the permanence of nature, the unchanging and basically unchangeable sea. Lest all of this sound too pessimistic let us remember that some plays will stress the benevolent or mutually beneficial relationship between man and nature.

Man and Society. While given assumption that all playwrights of any significance have something to say about "man", the other half of the thematic equation changes. Thus, many plays address themselves to the nature of the relationship between man and society. Sometimes this is done in timeless, universal terms—stating, for example, that man always has, presently does, and always will hate society because it restricts his freedom of personal action. Other times the theme will be more timely: the playwright will direct our attention to the relationship between man and the particular contemporary society in which the playwright and audience presently live. In a play we have considered previously, the eighteenth century play by Goldsmith, *She Stoops to Conquer*, there are numerous references to the relationship between man and contemporary society. Goldsmith's central attitude is that his society is presently too much absorbed in vanity and affectation, and that the ills of the city are slowly working their way out to the country, particularly as country people acquire the habit of taking trips to town for improving their fashion, hairdo, manners, styles, etc. Goldsmith is willing to make the opening lines of the play direct our immediate attention to the thematic implications:

> *Mrs. Hardcastle*: I vow, Mr. Hardcastle, you're very particular. Is there a creature in the whole country, but ourselves, that does not take a trip to town, now and then, to rub off the rust a little? There's the two Miss

Hoggs, and our neighbour Mrs. Grigsby, go to take a month's polishing every winter.

Hardcastle: Ay, and bring back vanity and affectation to last them the whole year. I wonder why London cannot keep its own fools at home. In my time the follies of the town crept slowly among us, but now they travel faster than a stagecoach.

If we were writing an essay interpreting *She Stoops to Conquer* we would necessarily need to explain Goldsmith's attitudes toward man and society. The entire plot is designed to accuse, though lightly, the vanity and social affectations of the age. The fact that Marlow finds Kate Hardcastle attractive only when she dresses and behaves like freewheeling barmaid is offered as evidence that vanity and affectation have elevated people too far; to be successful, to "conquer", it is necessary for Kate—and others, by implication—to "stoop". Goldsmith supplements the plot by continuous direct statement against the social foibles of "the age", making it explicitly a play about man and "contemporary" society.

Universal Themes of an Abstract Nature. The relationships between man and society and between man and nature can be discussed in fairly concrete terms; other themes are more abstract and our interpretations of them are also therefore more abstract. It is difficult to discuss death as a theme in anything other than abstract terms. For example, recalling another play we have examined, O'Neill's *The Iceman Cometh*, the theme is, basically, that death itself cometh, that death is unavoidable. Now this is hardly a new idea, but nevertheless it is an abstract one. We cannot avoid our private interpretations of the finality of death and yet we must somehow make a confrontation primarily with O'Neill's ideas on the subject. Throughout the play there are numerous references to the way in which the citizens of Harry Hope's bar spend their time constructing pipedreams; all are convinced that tomorrow will be better and nobody seems aware of the inevitable total of those tomorrows: death. Making Harry's last name "Hope", naming another character "Jimmy Tomorrow", and making constant reference to private pipedreams, O'Neill directs our attention to the irony with which most people approach death. We in the audience, but not the characters themselves, realize that they are being led to death, little by little, drink by drink, and unfulfilled pipedream by unfulfilled pipedream. Our interpretation of the play is that it is one dealing with the finality of death, yes, but also with unrealistic ways in which people, particularly unsuccessful people, prepare (or, in effect, do not prepare) for that death.

Death is of course not the only universal theme of an abstract nature. We can interpret plays having to do with freedom (a very abstract concept), morality, love, and all of the emotions which connect to these such as hate, revenge, jealousy, possessiveness, etc. While we can talk about Shakespeare's ideas on love as they are presented in the romantic comedy *A Midsummer Night's Dream*, we cannot make definite conclusions of a concrete sort. Love is not something that can be talked about as a single, recognizable object; in fact, one of the points of the play, one we would emphasize in interpreting it, is that there are many different kinds of love, all similar in some respects and dissimilar in others.

Family Relationships. There are countless plays that are aimed at the delineation of common human relationships, particularly those between particular members of particular families. How easy it is to discuss the relationship between Shakespeare's Coriolanus and his mother Volumnia, but how difficult to go from there to an interpretation of the play's central attitudes toward mother-son relationships in particular. Our interpretation of a play is strongly based on the action which transpires; what happens in the play is our largest clue to what the play means. And yet when we are interpreting that action we are likely to draw different conclusions from those drawn by someone else interpreting the action. Nevertheless there are certain universal patterns of family relationships such as the harmfully possessive mother, the jealous brother, etc. and our interpretation of a play can be made more accurate often simply by considering whether or not a particular family relationship is typical or highly different.

There are some themes which only concern themselves with very special family relationships. Incest, for example, is an atypical dramatic problem. A play dealing with incest and delineating a theme having to do with that incest is immediately a special kind of play. While it may be generally similar to other plays, as long as its theme is unconventional it maintains an unalterable difference. If a play chooses to present a story of several people in a family who relate in a peculiar way, that play is making use of a special family relationship. For example, Ibsen's famous and long-praised play *Ghosts* is a domestic tragedy and therefore generally similar to other domestic tragedies such as Heywood's late Renaissance play *A Woman Killed with Kindness*. Heywood's play covers the usual range of domestic tragedy in that there is the unfaithful wife and the wronged husband. In contrast, Ibsen's *Ghosts* is concerned with a very private kind of unusual family relationship. In order to demonstrate an uncommon theme—that the sins of the father are almost literally inherited by the son—Ibsen presents the strange fate of Oswald Alving. Because his father had syphilis, Oswald goes insane. In Ibsen's day this medical heredity was believed in religiously. The entire play is devoted to the ideas of disillusionment, to the father's sins, only to show their culmination in Oswald's final insanity at the end of the play. Oswald had never known that his father had been an unfaithful husband, much less that he had fathered the Alving's maid, whom Oswald would like to have married before he learned of her history. And yet Oswald is not as disappointed in his father as his mother, the widow Alving, had suspected. Oswald explains that he had not really known his father very well; in this statement of course is embodied all of the irony of the theme: not only does the son inherit the father's sins, but more often he inherits them from a father whom he hardly knows. The special situation of the play is that Oswald had not asked for the life he has been given. He begs his mother to kill him because after all it is only fair for her to take away something he never wanted. All in all, Ibsen translates the theme into a continuous nightmare. Our interpretation of the play involves both an explanation of the central theme—the son inherits the father's sins—and an explanation of the special way (device) by means of which this theme is made logical and graphic—the father's unfortunate syphilis which leads to a son's insanity. The play is based on a very special and unusual series of family relationships; Parson Manders had once courted Mrs. Helen (Alving) before her marriage and now consoles and hears confess; Oswald would like to marry his father's bastard; Mrs. Alving would like to live out her life in the exclusive company of her beloved son. There is a special strain in the relationships between the members of this particular family which is not easily discoverable in the relationships between members of ordinary families.

Other Private Themes. It is not only in family relationships that we find unusual, private themes demonstrated in particular ways. Major themes—such as the loss of innocence —and minor ones—such as in *Ghosts*—are found in different kinds of plays. Ibsen's *Ghosts* is a domestic tragedy, but the same theme can be found in early classical tragedies. The main point to remember is that some themes are more common than others; when we find a play which seems to us different in its meaning and intentions from other plays which we have read, we should try to locate the reasons for that difference in our interpretation of the play. If it is a play about love, why is it different in its implications from other plays about love. If it is a play about the brevity of life, how does it depart from other plays in the same vein. In other words, part of our interpretation must automatically be based upon the degree of conventionality in the play, for if the play explores a conventional theme—though in unusual ways—it will be easier for us to explain the action and to give a general account of the playwright's intentions.

John Gay's immortal eighteenth century comedy *The Beggar's Opera* which is several kinds of play all rolled into one—burlesque of an Italian Opera, satire on comedy of manners, parody of romance, etc. it takes in its central theme an unusual stance: marriage is a nuisance and a bothersome alliance between the sexes. The parents of the new bride are concerned in the very beginning of the play only with the fact that she is married; anything else, they feel, would be acceptable to them. Marriage is the main source of unhappiness and the play tries to make this abundantly clear. Macheath the highwayman has gone out of his way to marry quite a few women, at least in private if not in the eyes of the law. At the end of the play he is sentenced to what is humorously seen as the traditional "fate worse than death"—to stay married to one and only woman for the rest of his life. While the play is a comedy, and therefore not seriously criticizing marriage as an institution, it is nevertheless built upon the foundation of an unusual theme, that marriage is bad. We may say that perhaps the major theme of this play is criminals and the policemen are in league with each other.

Elements of Autobiography. Some plays are to be interpreted to a certain extent as autobiographical statements. The play will have plot which may be independent of the autobiography but nevertheless the playwright's personal involvement in one or more of the characters will force us to interpret the play in relationship to that playwright's involvement. More often than not a play of this kind may be interpreted both independently of the autobiographical elements and in the light of them. The important aspect of our task, nevertheless, is to suggest that two such interpretations are possible.

Miltion's *Samson Agonistes*. Milton's seventeenth century drama *Samson Agonistes* has been a popular play for several centuries. Many of those who read the play consider it in the light of its formal history—the first Greek tragedy in English. Others consider it purely from the perspective of the Bible. Milton has obviously chosen his story from the *Book of Judges* and yet many critics have found more parallels to the *Book of Job*, particularly as oppression is heaped upon Samson. Some interpret the play from the standpoint of contemporary Puritan politics, making *Samson Agonistes* more or less the locus of Milton's unleashing of his personal hostility toward political rivals. As an account of the growth of man in a spiritual sense, the play aptly follows Samson's tour through misery and suffering, on to a heroic conflict and final victory. The play is about the inward struggle of Samson but is it, as many have suggested, about the inner struggle of John Milton? To what extent, in other words, should our interpretation of the play consider the elements of autobiography? Is the theme of inward struggle and victory an autobiographical theme? One of the main arguments supporting the importance of interpreting the play in a biographical light derives from the fact that as the play opens Samson is blind—just as Milton was blind. When Samson complains of his despair and his blindness we have difficulty rejecting its associations with Milton's blindness; is the poet or the character speaking when Samson laments:

> O loss of sight, of thee I most complain!
> Blind among enemies, O worse than chains,
> Dungeon, or beggary, or decrepit age!
> Light the prime work of God to me is extinct,
> And all her various objects of delight
> Annull'd which might in part my grief have eas'd,
> Inferior to the vilest now become
> Of man or worm; the vilest here excel me,
> They creep, yet see; I dark in light expos'd
> To daily fraud, contempt, abuse and wrong,
> Within doors, or without, still as a fool,
> In power of others, never in my own;
> Scarce half I seem to live, dead more than half.
> O dark, dark, dark, amid the blaze of noon,
> Irrecoverably dark, total Eclipse
> Without all hope of day! (ll. 67-82)

The general tone of Samson's speech make us realize how well understood is the experience of blindness; the passage must be taken as possibly autobiographical. The reference to being blind among enemies, furthermore, would suggest Milton's bitterness over political alienation. Furthermore, throughout the play we find the continuous development of a theme of Milton's life—what is strength without wisdom? At one point Samson expresses another Miltonic attitude—that friends are scarce when they are most needed; Samson notes that "in prosperous days/ They swarm, but in adverse withdraw their head/ Not to be found through sought." Such remarks throughout the play suggest all of Milton's personal disappointment in his later life, while at the same time there is, through Samson, his equal feeling of eventual triumph over personal despair which must be discussed both in general terms, adhering with some rigidity to the story of Samson as it is related in the Book of Judges, and in private terms, adhering to some extent to the facts of Milton's personal life as they correspond to the events in Samson's life.

Historical Background. Without going into any extensive analysis of a play's historical background at this point, let us at least suggest that sometimes our interpretation of a play will address itself to that very background. Just as when we have elements of autobiography to consider, sometimes we have historical facts and events upon which we must focus. If we were inclined toward making a political interpretation of Milton's play, for example, we would have to read into it (or out of it) the entire set of political facts of the time, explaining Milton's party affiliations and the chronology of Puritan politics of the day. Sometimes it is almost impossible to interpret a play without understanding and explaining the historical background against which it was written and which it still reflects. No reading of Marlowe's *Dr. Faustus*, or its thematic predecessor Robert Greene's *Friar Bacon and Friar Bungay* could be complete without some understanding of the prevailing contemporary views of scholarship on the one hand and necromancy on the other. No interpretation of O'Neill's *The Iceman Cometh* would be valid without some acknowledgement of the conditions prevailing in the locale of the play at the time when the action is supposedly taking place: the Lowest West side of New York City has peculiar characteristics which foster the development of despair and futile pipedreams; without relating Rocky and his two prostitutes to this environment we can at best offer only a partial interpretation of the play. An essential aspect of our interpretation is the development (even if brief) of the historical landscape against which the play has been written. Neither Shakespeare's *The Merchant of Venice* nor Marlowe's *The Jew* *of Malta* could be skilfully explained without some reference to the contemporary Elizabethan attitudes toward Jewish people, even a slight play like Ben Jonson's quasi-masque, *The Gipsies Metamorphosed*, would not make sense without at least a minimal explanation of the image of gypsies at the time when the play was written.

All and all, then, we should always suggest the historical implications of the theme, even if we do not want to make the historical background our major consideration. In O'Neill's play we are ultimately concerned with the finality of death, the meaning of death, and man's preparations for death. We want to mention the world of the play in time and space, though, in order to make our interpretation more complete. In Marlowe's *Dr. Faustus* we want to explore the theme that ruin results from bartering with evil, but at the same time we cannot completely ignore the intellectual experience which the play records. While we put meaning first on our list, we nevertheless consider other aspects in order to round out our total interpretation. The main theme in Ibsen's *Ghosts* is that the sins of the father are inherited by the son; this is our main concern. We want to discuss this theme and explain how Ibsen makes it come alive; and yet we must mention—if not extensively explain—that the contemporary opinion was that syphilis did have hereditary characteristics. The sins could literally be inherited by the son; we are not dealing simply with an abstract theme.

Interpretation as Audience Conception. Our interpretation of a play is basically our own conception of the play, i.e. although we can discuss the playwright's intentions, can establish the theme as one dealing, say, with relationship between man and his society, finally we must explain our own conception of the play. First we consider the ways in which we feel affected by the play and then we try to explain why are affected in these particular ways. Sometimes we have undeniable personal associations with the action or characters of a play; we are reminded of events or attitudes in our own lives. We have, in other words, some subjective involvement in the world of the play which almost automatically colours our conception of the play as a work of art.

Often it is worthwhile to make a "far-out" interpretation of the play. By assigning the action of the play a bizarre meaning and then demonstrating this point of view as it is translated by the characters, we are often forced into accepting the more conventional interpretation of the play. In short, we strive to be contrary, to go against the prevailing ideas about the play in order to discover whether our own true feelings support or deny the popular views. By seeking to be different we may be forced to agree with the conventional, but we are much more secure in this conventionality for our having attempted first to reject it. Lest this sounds as if we are inevitably driven to the popular conclusions, we should emphasize perhaps that some of the very best literary criticism that has opened new doors to interpretation has deliberately sought out the unconventional with great success. By searching for the least obvious implications of a drama we sometimes are led to an entirely new system of philosophy behind the play. Our conception of the play may then acquire great importance as well as enviable validity in the eyes of other readers. Our usual avenue of approach is simply to say, this is not a play about X at all; it is really an extended debate over Y. Then we attempt to show that the playwright has tried to present an unusual view of something while at the same time directing our immediate attention to something more obvious or immediate. If it turns out that we are wrong, we can make our conclusion nevertheless: this is not in anyway a play about Y but rather is, a several other critics have maintained, a play about X. When we try to find that Y is under discussion we are continuously forced to admit that X is really the playwright's central concern.

Our final conception of the play as a work of art, as a structured presentation of major ideas, must, above all, be imaginative. This is what we are really suggesting when we say that it is worthwhile to attempt, even with the exception of failure, to make some kind of "far-out" interpretation. For although we can understand the playwright's basic intentions, the major shifts in action as they relate to his ideas, nevertheless we will write a dull analysis unless we use some imagination to seek for other, possible (even if unlikely) ways of understanding the play.

8

Evaluation and Criticism

"Criticism" is the term we use to designate the description, analysis, and judgment of literary works of art. Criticism covers all the activities with which we have been concerned throughout this book; however, our attention is now more specifically directed toward "total evaluation". What, in a final analysis, is our view of a play? What sort of criticism can we write about it (note that criticism does not have any negative connotations when we used in literary evaluation; criticism can be entirely positive, for the term as here used does not imply finding fault but rather finding skills)? There are several basic distinctions which should be kept in mind when we discuss criticism. There is no point in our tracing the evolution of literary criticism in all of its complexity and copiousness, but we need to understand several related terms.

Aristotelian and Platonic. Two basic kinds of criticism are Aristotelian and the Platonic. We associate Aristotle with formal, logical analysis of works of art: the standards are severe and exceptions to rules are not treated lightly. Furthermore, because there are formal guidelines to what a work of art should be, the Aristotelian critic is able to discover the basic value of that work within it. The play's meaning is entirely self-contained and we need not seek outside the play for any understanding of its values. Platonic criticism, in contrast, suggests a utilitarian attitude toward works of art. A play's value is the practical good it brings to people; art, in this perspective, is less formal, but morally stimulating; the value of the play is seen more in the effect it has on the audience than in its artistic value. The play is insignificant/worthless until allowed to become a force, a didactic force in fact, for the perpetuation of moral harmony. Thus, the basic dichotomy between Aristotelian and Platonic criticism is that one is inner-directed and the other is outer-directed. The distinction is a good one to bear in mind when evaluating a play because it allows the student to achieve (if he so desires) an immediate double-barreled view of a play simply by asking two questions: Is the play a work of art, an independent criticism? Does it derive its power and value from the great effect it has upon the audience?

Relativistic and Absolutist. A closely related and less important distinction is that between relativistic and absolutist criticism. The relativistic critic feels strongly that any and all standards of evaluation may logically be applied to a play as a work of art; the goal of understanding is placed significantly above the formality of the means; if the play can be better understood through the use of an unconventional system of analysis, the end inevitably justifies the means. The absolutist critic, in contradiction, holds to one system of analysis with dogmatic rigidity. The absolutist critic feels equally strongly that there is only one established critical procedure to works of art and he adheres to that procedure with admirable (if sometimes detestable) tenacity.

Theoretical and Practical. Another useful distinction to bear in mind is that between theoretical criticism—designed to arrive at general theories about works of literature—and practical criticism—designed to use such theories in the interpretation of individual works of art. In effect, the former kind of criticism moves from the particular to the general by moving from the individual play to theories about all plays, while the latter moves from the general to the particular by moving from theories about plays in general to the way in which these theories are seen operative in particular plays. For the most part, students will need to concentrate on the merits of the particular play and leave the formulation of theories to more experienced critics. This is not said to discourage but rather to warn the students to think twice before sailing into the jumbled waters of theoretical dramatic criticism.

THE CRITIC'S PURPOSE/AIM

The kind of criticism of a play which we write will to some extent be dictated by our purpose. In general, of course, we want to arrive at an evaluation of a play, but sometimes our assigned or self-defined purpose is given a particular emphasis: do we want to justify a certain kind of drama, show that it contains as much imagination and value as more conventional, accepted kinds of drama? Or do we want to pass judgment on a play according to a specific set of rules? For example, is our purpose to judge the play primarily, or even exclusively, in terms of Aristotle's rules for the composition of drama outlined in his *Poetics*? Are we basically making an attempt to discover and explain what the springs of dramatic excitement or tension are? In short, our exact purpose will colour the kind of criticism which we undertake. If we are setting out to make a general criticism of the play—which is often the case—there is no need to explain that this is our purpose; on the other hand, any particular intentions should be clearly explained in our opening paragraph. Now that certain distinctions have been explained, and the importance of stating one's intentions has been emphasized, we can pass on to a series of questions which we should ask about a play.

What Kind of Play is it Supposed to be? It is obvious that our very first question should direct our attention to the intentions of the playwright; how futile and even infantile it would be to interpret a comedy by systems of analysis we might use in discussing tragedy. Thus, the student should always begin (following a statement of his own intentions) by mentioning what kind of play it is supposed to be, for this leads to the next general question.

Does it Meet the General Requirements of this Kind of Play? Our major perspective of evaluation has to do with what is "appropriate" in drama, i.e. does a play meet the requirements which we generally make for plays of this kind?

If, for example, we have a domestic tragedy, we note briefly that one of the requirements of a domestic tragedy is that the hero or protagonist of the play be an ordinary, common sort of person, and then we note whether the author of the play in question follows this requirement. If we are examining Addison's *Cato*, for example, which is supposed to be a classical tragedy, we would need to explain the ways in which Addison has carefully adhered to the requirements of classical tragedy—that there is unity of place, that all of the action takes place within a twenty-four-hour day, that there is unity of action, that a person of noble stature falls from a high to a low estate, etc. We evaluate the play, in other words, in relationship to the things we know about this kind of play. This exemplifies a kind of practical criticism, for we move from statements about the kind of play in general to statements about the particular play in question, all for the purpose of evaluating it first in terms of what kind of play it claims to be.

Are the Playwright's Intentions Stated, and Does He Achieve them? Aside from the intended major kind of play which the dramatist is purportedly composing, there are other intentions which can be noted. Again, our cardinal principle is to evaluate in the right way. In other words, if the playwright is trying, either directly or indirectly, to produce a certain effect, we must evaluate the play to a certain extent by way of describing the success with which that effect is (or is not) achieved. The dramatist wants, for example, to force us to consider the meaning of death (*The Iceman Cometh*). Because he makes it clear that this is his intention we must, as critics, respond to his intention first. While the play may achieve accidental results, that is produce effects which the playwright may not have counted on, our primary aim is to evaluate the success of the author's intentions. Has the playwright produced the effect which he set out to produce? Has he stimulated us intellectually into a consideration of ideas which he wants us to consider? Is the playwright obviously striving to depress us? He is writing the play for specific reasons and part of these reasons, at least, must come into our judgment of the work. If the play is not very entertaining—is not, therefore, good drama

—but nevertheless achieves the playwright's goal, how do we evaluate the play? We can and must point out that the dramatist has apparently accomplished what he set out to do, but that the resulting play is not very interesting or entertaining. The final evaluation will probably be that the playwright succeeded in conception but failed in execution; that is, he wrote the play in the right way in terms of what was planned, yet made a mistake in that very planning. One reason, therefore, that we need to at least make a short consideration of the playwright's various intentions is that they may form the one "saving" aspect of the play. We cannot totally condemn a play which at least succeeds in intention, even when the conception of it is poor.

How do We Measure Other Kinds of Achievement? Our estimation of a playwright's success operates on as many different levels as we have elements of interpretation/analysis. Everything subject to interpretation/analysis becomes automatically subject to evaluation. Thus, we can and usually should evaluate the playwright's achievement in regard to character, to action, to language, to diction, to structure and to meaning. If upon analysis characters are found to be what we have previously defined as "thematic characters", we must judge the success with which the playwright has made these characters consistent with the themes which they represent. If Iago is the personification of evil, for example, and does some good act in the play (he does not), he may be an inconsistently developed character. Perhaps consistency is the key to all of our evaluation. Characters should act "in character"; this is not a tautology but rather a way of emphasizing the necessity that a character's actions be (i) consistent with one another; (ii) consistent with the character's beliefs; and (iii) consistent with what we are told about that character by other characters.

In short, consistently cannot be too strongly underlined as the point of departure for most of our criticism of a play. We are always concerned with measuring the playwright's achievement, and one of the ways in which this can be done is to describe how the playwright has consistently had character X act in a certain way, how the various characters speak in the same general language throughout the play (rather than, say, speaking low language one minute and high language the next without any logical explanation of the change), how the structure of the play has been given unity, how the parts of the play have been connected, how the theme emerges from the events of the play. In the final analysis/interpretation (we review the steps in the final chapter) of a play we must try to piece together the various ways in which the playwright has or has not been consistent. We cannot tolerate the yoking of different kinds of language or inconsistent actions without at least some kind of accompanying explanation.

THE SPECIFIC MERITS OF THE PLAY OR THE PLAYWRIGHT

A large part of any formal criticism is the explanation of the specific merits of either the play or the playwright in question. When we can carefully measure the success of the play in terms of the playwright's implied or stated intentions, it remains to point out what is unique about the play. What, we inquire, are the specific merits of this play? And often, of course, we must conclude that there are not specific merits at all, that the play is common and also typical of its type. This is often the case when we examine the conventional plays of minor playwrights: the play which is only a poor imitation of one of Dryden's heroic dramas or of Shakespeare's early comedies. Most critical statements of major significance, however, contain reference to the uniqueness of the playwright. Perhaps it is the way in which the playwright allows the plot to develop in an extremely slow and mysterious way, perhaps it is the way in which the playwright captures the language of common conversation among people in real life; this, for example, was one of the views expressed by Dr. Johnson on Shakespeare in his *Preface to Shakespeare*. One of the most important critical statements in all literature, Johnson's Preface alludes specifically to Shakespeare's particular ability to capture language neither overly rude nor overly refined:

> If there be, what I believe there is, in every nation, a stile which never becomes obsolete, a certain mode of phraseology so consonant and congenial to the analogy and principles of its respective language as to remain

> settled and unaltered; this style is probably to be sought in the common intercourse of life, among those who speak only to be understood, without ambition of elegance. The polite are always catching modish innovations, and the learned depart from established forms of speech, in hopes of finding or making better; those who wish for distinction forsake the vulgar, when the vulgar is right; but there is a conversation above grossness and below refinement, where propriety resides, and where this poet (Shakespeare) seems to have gathered his comick dialogue. He is therefore more agreeable to the ears of the present age than any other author equally remote, and among his other excellencies deserves to be studied as one of the original masters of our language.

Johnson has pointed out, as a critic, what he feels to be one of Shakespeare's particular merits. Every critic must attempt to make some kind of similar presentation with regard to the particular merits of a play or playwright.

Keeping in mind some of the plays with which we have been concerned throughout this book, what are some of the particular merits which come to mind. In Miller's *Death of a Salesman* we are inclined to emphasize how skilfully Miller has given the effects of classical tragedy to a bourgeois tragedy. There is no high or noble hero; Willy Loman, however, seems to suffer in as serious a way as do the heroes of Sophocles. In Synge's *Riders to the Sea* we emphasize the use of an excellent idiom throughout the play; one of Synge's outstanding characteristics as a playwright is his ability to capture the precise sound of the conversation of the simple Irish folk-people living on islands off the coast of Ireland. In Gay's *Beggar's Opera* we noted the unique theme used for comic thrust and in *She Stoops to Conquer* the excellence with which Goldsmith reflects the manners and social foibles of his own age; in *Midsummer Night's Dream* the expert way in which Shakespeare contrasts kinds of language through Theseus, Bottom, Puck, etc. and so forth. In each instance we have—perhaps almost unconsciously—addressed ourselves to the particular merits of the play as well as to the conventional lines of development of character, structure, meaning, language, and style in general.

THE THEME IN RELATIONSHIP TO THE KIND OF PLAY

A final consideration is whether or not the play is the right kind of vehicle for conveying the particular theme. Can an overly serious accusation of government really be successfully conveyed in a low comedy; can humour be successful—even though only comic-relief—in a high tragedy. In other words, granted that the playwright has successfully conveyed his stated theme, has, in other words, achieved his desired goal, we can still pass judgment on whether or not he has chosen the right kind of play. The point is not to say, "This theme might have been better presented in another kind of play"; we are not generally inclined to seek negative conclusions as part of our criticism. Thus, our real orientation is more along the lines of, "This is the right kind of play to present his particular theme because...." We are looking for the proper explanation of the dramatist's choice; we are trying to explain, as we must in literary criticism of any sort, the relationship between form and content, or between technique and meaning. If criticism is to be constructive—and any that is not is more or less meaningless—there must be some attempt to discuss the form of the play, the kind of play, and the intentions of the play in their overall relationship to the requirements of this kind of play. We must pay particular attention to both the conventional aspects of execution and to the particular merits of the play. In the final chapter we will review the basic ways in which we can analyze/interpret a play and relate them to this final act of summarized criticism.

9

Presenting an Analysis

This chapter is designed to be a review of the methods of interpretation/analysis which we have discussed throughout this study. The goal of this chapter is to show how the various aspects of interpretation/analysis may be synthesized into a coherent total examination of a play.

Initial Decisions. Before even lifting his pen—or taking key-board in the hand, in deference to modernity—the student should make several initial decisions. The first is the length of the analysis: how long is the paper going to be? The second develops out of the answer to the first: how many aspects of analysis will I have the time to include? Another basic decision has to do with emphasis. In any given interpretation/analysis of a play a writer will necessarily have to emphasize some aspects of interpretation/analysis more than others. Once the writer has decided how many aspects he will include, he then needs them to arrange them in a particular order designed to reflect his intended emphasis. He should also combine these to show them as parts/ features of a unified approach.

Establishing the Components of Your Interpretation/ Analysis. Once these initial decisions have been made the student should select the areas of interpretation/analysis which he wants to cover and then arrange them in an effective order. For example, the student may design his essay to correspond to the following paragraph topics:

1. Definition of the world of the play.
2. Explanation of the importance of the major characters.
3. Explanation of the significance of the action of these characters.
4. The ways in which these actions are interwoven.
5. How this process of interweaving allows for the gradual development of the major theme of the play.
6. Further interpretation of this theme.
7. Conclusion relating the characters to the theme in a summary statement; final evaluation of the effectiveness with which the playwright has connected characters to the theme.

In this seven-paragraph essay the student has placed the emphasis on character without making the interpretation/analysis too exclusively concerned with character. Discussion of the atmosphere of the play is incorporated into the first paragraph; the translation of character's attitudes into action is handled in the third paragraph; the relationship between action and theme in the fourth, and so forth. The point is that the student has selected the components of his interpretation/analysis in a way designed to include various aspects of interpretation/analysis while at the same time giving central importance to only one area of interpretation/analysis. It follows that his final criticism of the play will address itself primarily to the playwright's development of the characters; by considering the characters in their relationship to action, meaning, etc. the student is able to enlarge his critical perspective and form reliable opinions on the characters in general.

Other Arrangements of Components. In all expository writing, attention is given to the "order" of presentation of ideas. In writing an interpretation/analysis of a play we must consider the various ways of ordering our aspects of interpretation/analysis. After selecting the aspects which we will cover (as determined by our allotted length, objectives, etc.), we must consider possible ways of ordering these aspects.

For example, let us suppose that we want to write a fairly long paper—may be twenty pages—which would interpret/analyze a play both with reference to its formal aspects—structure, design, rhetoric—and to its possible meanings. What sort of order do we plan? Well, in the first place, it is obvious that we need to begin by stating our intention of interpreting/analyzing the play in two basic ways—technically and thematically. As we are more likely to cover the basic events of the play—what happens—it follows logically that it would be more sensible to begin with the formal aspects and move to the informal, speculative interpretations. As here we want to interpret/analyse how the form and the technique of the play embody the meaning and the vision of the author.

After deciding which half of our interpretation/analysis comes first, we need to order our material within each half. Probably it would be good idea to begin with the structure of the play, then proceed to the characters, their actions, and their speech. In this way, each aspect grows out of the preceding one. In our second half of the paper, that dealing with the possible meanings of the play, we would probably do well to follow what is known as the climactic order. That is, we plan our order of presentation of different interpretations so that it will climax with the interpretation which we favour above all the others. This means that we will first present some typical and conventional interpretations of the play, follow these with one or two "far-out" or wild interpretations, then "climax" with the interpretation which we favour. Our full interpretation/analysis thus would look like this:

(a) Statement that we will interpret/analyze the play in two basic ways to show how they are interrelated.

(b) Formal interpretation/analysis:

   (i) The structure of the play

   (ii) The characters

   (iii) The actions of the characters

   (iv) The rhetorical usage of the characters

(c) The interpretation of the play (now that we are fully acquainted with what happens in the play, what the characters are like, etc.)
   (i) Most common interpretation
   (ii) Other conventional interpretations
   (iii) A few more unconventional, "far-out" interpretations
   (iv) The interpretation which we think is the most accurate, its essential difference from the conventional interpretations, the relating of this interpretation to the formal considerations in B.

It follows that we might be supporting rather than attacking a conventional interpretation of the play; if this were the case we would present some of the unconventional interpretations of the play and demonstrate their fallacies (presuming there are some fallacies), then present the conventional view of the play which we feel is closer to the true meaning and to the playwright's intentions.

General pattern of ordering are as follows: from easy to more complex aspects of interpretation/analysis, from usual to unusual aspects, from standard rhetorical-style examples to special, peculiar rhetorical-style examples, from structure to character, from character to action, from action (event) to theme, from theme to interpretation. Usually it is more logical to reverse your order that is deal first with the themes and then with the form. Unless we are writing an essay designed to be criticism exclusively, we will order our components in such a way as to have them culminate in our criticism. We can cover the areas of interpretation/analysis by presenting the facts, or answers to basic questions: How is the play designed? What do the characters do in the play? What is the basic meaning of their actions? Then, after answering these questions in relatively brief ways, we can move that part of our paper reserved for criticism. Here we will take up some—but probably not all—of the aspects which we have covered, work upon the assumption that our reader already knows the essential facts about these aspects, and explain why we do or do not find them successful aspects in both planning and execution. Criticism, in other words, should not have to stop and explain anything basic about the play or its various aspects; rather, criticism takes it for granted that the reader knows all of the essential facts about the play and is now interested in listening to someone's evaluation or judgment of what is already known.

The Basic Pattern of Interpretation/Analysis. We have explained the probable ordering of components of interpretation/analysis as determined by particular objectives. Now it remains only to remind the reader of what we might call the basic pattern of interpretation/analysis. Essentially the progression should correspond to the table of contents of this book; reduced to the minimum of terms, this means that the full interpretation/analysis of a play would treat the following subjects in this order:

(1) An introduction to the paper explaining that this is to be a critical analysis of all aspects of the play in order to show how the meaning is reflected in the form of the play. Perhaps hint here at the conclusions you will reach.

(2) Definition of the world of the play—its location, atmosphere, emotional framework, etc.

(3) Explanation of the structure of the play. How the play is logically divided into parts? How are these parts connected?

(4) Discussion of the characters (amount of time you spend on each character should correspond to that character's importance).

(5) The language and rhetoric of the play; then discussion of figurative language, in particular, any use of irony, reversals, etc.

(6) Interpretations of the play, emphasis on your own view of the play, even if it is largely similar to that of another critic.

(7) Evaluation and criticism; this forms, in effect, the conclusion to your paper and should stand not as an isolated component but rather as the crowning section of your paper, to some extent dependent upon, and to some extent a summary of everything else in your paper.

With this total scheme in mind, the student should be able to make a logical and interesting interpretation/analysis of a play. The combination of aspects of interpretation/analysis will result in a good paper as long as there is no disproportion of emphasis; that is, too much discussion of one aspect of interpretation/analysis at the expense of others and ultimately all the aspects are integrated into a unified approach to the work.

Glossary

Act. A major division of a play (or opera). On the contemporary stage, the three-act play is most common. In classical theory, a play was divided into five acts. This was generally maintained until the late 19th century, when the last two acts were compressed and the four-act play was produced (Chekhov). In modern times playwrights began to write one-act plays and these are now recognized as a separate genre.

Action. The events that take place in a work of literature. Though critics employ the term "action" to refer to the series or succession of events that together form the plot of a play or narrative, a distinction may be made between the physical and psychological action, consisting of a character's internal conflicts or the clash of wills between characters. Aristotle says that action is basic in the drama. External action comprises those physical movements that actually take place in relation to the characters. Internal action refers to a character's thoughts and feelings as they are reported to the audience.

Alienation Effect. see Epic Theatre.

Antagonist. From the Greek *antagonistes*, meaning an opponent. Generally (s)he is the major character in opposition to the hero or protagonist of a play or narrative. In Shakespeare's *Othello*, for example, Othello is the protagonist and Iago is the antagonist.

Anti-Hero. A type of hero who has none of the qualities traditionally associated with heroes. He lacks the traditional heroic qualities (such as courage, idealism, vigor, etc.). He is frequently a pathetic, comic, or even antisocial figure. The anti-hero finds commitment to ideals difficult or impossible because of his sense of helplessness in a world over which he has no control or whose values he suspects. Willy Loman, in Arthur Miller's *Death of a Salesman* (1949), and Jimmy Porter, in John Osborne's *Look Back in Anger* (1956), are examples of anti-heroes.

Antimasque. A grotesque or farcical interlude, usually humorous dance, interspersed among the beautiful and serious actions and dances of a masque. Often performed by professional dancers, the antimasque served as a foil to the masque proper, performed by courtly amateurs. The development (and possibly the origin) of the antimasque is due to Ben Jonson.

Black Comedy. A type of drama based on the belief that human beings exist in a meaningless and purposeless universe in which they are subject to forces beyond their control or understanding. So the characters act without motive and the events occur without any cause. Moreover these events are often simultaneously comic, horrifying, and absurd as the humour arises from a pathetic or unhappy context/situation. Moral and ethical values, therefore, are meaningless, and life is, in Ionesco's words, "a tragic farce". Examples of black comedy are Jean Genet's *The Maids* (1954), Harold Pinter's *The Homecoming* (1965), Joe Orton's *Entertaining Mr. Sloane* (1965).

Bourgeois Drama. A term applied to plays to describe the realistic drama dealing with the problems of middle-class characters. Such plays deal with the life of the common (middle-class) people rather than that of the courtly or the rich.

Chorus. In ancient Greece, the group of dancers and singers who participated in religious festivals and dramatic performances; the songs sung by the chorus. At first, the choral songs made up the major part of the play. As the Greek drama progressed, the role of the chorus altered and its importance diminished. In Aeschylus, the chorus often takes part in action; in Sophocles, it is a commentator; and in Euripides, the chorus is primarily a lyric element. Even as it comments on the action, the Romans borrowed the chorus from the Greeks. In Elizabethan drama, the role of the chorus was often taken by a single character, who recited the prologue and epilogue and commented on the action and informs the audience regarding the coming events. In Shakespeare's *Henry V*, the chorus comments on the action, explains scene changes and demands the audience for a sympathetic attitude. In modern plays, one can rarely find a chorus, but when they appear, they may be multiple, as in T.S. Eliot's *Murder in the Cathedral.* Sometimes, minor characters serve choric functions as in *The Family Reunion* and *Desire under the Elms.*

Chronicle Plays. A type of drama that flourished during the reign of Queen Elizabeth I (1533-1603). The term was influenced by the popular *Chronicles* (1578) of Raphael Holinshed, from which many stories and plots of the plays (*Macbeth, King Lear*) were taken. Such plays were very popular in Elizabethan England as they stressed the nationalistic spirit of the times. At first these plays were simply a series of scenes loosely strung together, but they soon developed greater unity and in such plays as Marlowe's *Edward II* and Shakespeare's *Henry IV* (also called 'history plays'), became subtle studies of character.

Climax. The highest or culminating point in a play at which a crisis reaches its highest intensity and is resolved. In dramatic structure, the term commonly means the moment of action that determines the turning point or reversal—the decisive moment in the dramatic conflict.

Closet Drama. A play especially written for reading rather than enacting on the stage. For example, Tennyson's *Becket* or Shelley's *Prometheus Unbound* have survived as literature rather than theatrical performances.

Comedy. A kind of drama that is primarily intended to entertain the audience, and that ends happily for the characters. The term is flexible enough to include the satirical laughter of Aristophanes, the religious exaltation of Dante, and near-tragedy of Chekhov. Comedy differs from farce and burlesque by having a more sustained plot, more weighty and subtle dialogue, more natural characters and less boisterous behaviour. However, the borderline between comedy and other dramatic forms cannot be sharply defined, as there is much overlapping of technique, and different forms are frequently combined.

Since comedy strives to amuse, both wit and humour are utilized. The range of appeal is wide, varying from the crude effects of low comedy, to the subtle and idealistic reactions aroused by some high comedy.

Comedy of Humours. A special type of comedy developed at the end of the Elizabethan period especially by Ben Jonson. Laughter (or the comic) is derived largely from the exhibition of "humorous" character—i.e. a person whose behaviour is controlled by some one characteristic or "humour". During the Renaissance, this term referred to the four fluids of the human body—blood, phlegm, yellow bile, and black bile. According to the theory of the time, physical diseases and moral temperaments were decided as per the level of these fluids in the body. When these fluids were in balance, an ideal temperament could be seen. Ben Jonson in his comedies—especially in his *Every Man in His Humours* (1598)—utilized the theory of humours.

Comedy of Manners. The type of comedy concerned with the manners, etiquettes and conventions of an artificial, highly sophisticated society. Characters in such comedies are, generally, types rather than individual characters, and their behaviour is more important than basic morality. Comedies written by Etherege, Congreve, Wycherley and others focus on foibles of certain people or society.

Comedy, Sentimental. Also called the "Drama of Sensibility". It is a kind of drama that appeared in the early eighteenth century in England in reaction to what was regarded as the immorality of the restoration comedy of manners. This type of play emphasized the distresses of middle-class characters in order to evoke the audience's sympathies. These plays depicted good and bad characters with so extraordinarily simplicity that they became caricatures. Virtue always triumphed. The hero may be absolutely magnanimous, always acting from a sense of honour, and acutely attuned to the sensibilities of others, including those on lower social levels. These specific elements of sentimental comedy developed from both theatrical and social changes at the end of the seventeenth century. In such plays dramatic reality was sacrificed in an attempt to instruct through an appeal to the audience's emotions.

Comic Relief. Comic elements, incidents, characters or speeches placed in a serious or somber work, especial a play, even a tragedy, to relieve its tension, widen its scope, or heighten by contrast the tragic emotion. The drunken porter scene in Shakespeare's *Macbeth* is a classic example of comic relief which brings back the world of normality after the murder of Duncan.

Comedia Dell'arte. A form of drama evolved in the 16th century Italy in which traveling companies of actors improvised comic plays around standard plots using stock characters. A typical play might involve a young lover, the "Inamarato", tricking "Pantaloon", a rich old father, into giving up his daughter. "Harlequin", the clever servant and "Punch" the clown were other stock types. The play was enlivened by dancing, singing and slapstick buffoonery. Many elements of the form are visible in comic plays by Shakespeare and Moliére.

Dramatis Personae. The characters in a play. Generally, a list of characters, with the description of their relationships, is printed at the beginning of the play.

Epic Theater. The theory and practice of the German dramatist Bertolt Brecht (1898-1956). In order to avoid Aristotelian idea of theater—creating the illusion of reality—Brecht tried to present "anti-Aristotelian" drama in which the audience could see the action with a peculiar detachment evoked by the original singers of epic. The goal of the epic theater is to lead the audience not to feel or experience but to make them think and evaluate critically the characters' actions as determined not by fate but by social circumstances. It aims to make audience leave the theater not emotionally drained but intellectually stimulated to bring about Marxist reforms. To achieve this effect of emotional distance between audience and action, called "Alienation Effect" or Estrangement effect (*Verfremdungseffekt*), Brecht used short scenes instead of building action to a climax used songs to comment on the action, and encouraged actors to avoid emotional identification with their roles and to play in a relaxed style.

Estrangement Effect. see Epic Theater.

Farce. Generally, it means low comedy, created only to evoke laughter through gestures, buffoonery, rough (coarse) wit, action or creation of ridiculous situations; and it is little concerned with subtlety of characterization and plot.

Poetic Drama. Poetic plays written to be acted. For example, T.S. Eliot's *Murder in the Cathedral* (1935).

Problem Play. Also known as "thesis play" or "propaganda play". A play in which a social problem is elucidated and a sort of solution is also suggested. It is also known as the drama of ideas. A Shaw play like *Mrs. Warren's Profession*, is an example. Ibsen and Galsworthy are some of the writers of such plays.

Revenge Tragedy. Also known as tragedy of blood. It is a popular form of drama during the Elizabethan period influenced by the Roman tragedian Seneca. Senecan plays offered a general model for a serious, passionate drama. In it appear such Senecan elements as ghosts, the theme of revenge, and lurid/sensational events (murder, mutilation, for example). This type of drama was made popular on the English stage by Thomas Kyd's *The Spanish Tragedy* (1592). The general theme of these plays is the revenge of the father for a murdered son or vice versa, and the revenge is directed by the ghost of a murdered person. Elements of such plays include procrastination of a hero, feigned madness, intrigue, scheming villain, the play within the play, soliloquies, on-stage violence. Shakespeare's *Hamlet* can be considered as a classic example of this type of drama.

Further Reading

Abrams, M.H. *A Glossary of Literary Terms*. 7th Ed. Singapore: Harcourt, 2001.

Esslin, Martin. *An Anatomy of Drama*. London: Temple Smith, 1976.

Styan, J.L. *Drama, Stage and Audience*. Cambridge: CUP, 1975.

Styan, J.L. *Elements of Drama*. Cambridge: CUP, 1960.

Styan, J.L. *Modern Drama Theory and Practice*. Cambridge: CUP, 1982.

Styan, J.L. *The Dramatic Experience: A Guide to the Reading of Plays*. Cambridge: CUP, 1975.